Advance Praise

"Here you have a man who strives to make the choice to love every day. He has powerfully transformed the adversity of his own childhood—first, into challenge, and then, into blessing for his own family and to an ever-growing number of others. Thanks to David Hirsch for seeing fatherhood as the vocation it is. Read this book! On every page, you will find the beauty of the difference that true-to-the-end dads make in the lives of their children."

—Rev. Marak Bartosic
Our Lady of Charity Parish & St. Frances of Rome Parish

"In this age, when single parent, female-led households are becoming the norm, we need voices like that of David Hirsch to continuously remind us of how essential it is to have a father present in every aspect of every child's life. In this book, the reader gets a taste of David's life-long advocacy, and the lessons learned along the way through the lens of his incredible 2,300 mile+ journey. Twenty-six years of being a father, and nineteen years of advocating for meaningful father involvement have come together to create one of the most important and inspirational works ever written about the true art of fatherhood."

—John Bellamy, entrepreneur

"David Hirsch's commitment to the cause of dads is not just a part-time interest. It is his identity. More than anything, he is a dad. As the father of five amazing children, he has proven in real life what a dad should and can be. His bike ride spanning over two thousand miles to raise awareness and funds brought him in close contact with numerous individuals on the way. This book recounts the stories that were shared and the memories that were made on that long journey. It will warm your heart and lift your spirit."

—Britto M. Berchmans, Pastor
St. Paul of the Cross Catholic Church

"Failure as a father is an option for far too many men in America. No one appreciates the loss our communities and families suffer more, and no one is more engaged and committed to finding a solution than David Hirsch. *21st Century Dads* tells his story as a son, the true story of fatherhood today, and his decades long initiatives to bring fathers into the lives of their children. He continues with a national campaign to promote local programs dedicated to engaging fathers and helping do the right thing with respect to their children."

—Greg Bishop, Founder
Boot Camp for New Dads

"In the Latino culture fathers have traditionally been protectors, providers, pathfinders and a strong presence. In these changing and complex times where women work outside the home and people no longer live in the communities where they were born, it is time to redefine and reinvigorate the role of father. This book shows the way for fathers to be more involved and to lead the way in creating healthy and happy families."

—Juana Bordas, best-selling author, *Salsa, Soul, and Spirit: Leadership for a Multicultural Age and The Power of Latino Leadership*

"David Hirsch is a mover and leader in the 'Fathering' movement. His personal commitment to his own family distinguishes him as an "overcomer" father, but in addition he is raising the importance of responsible fathering in the consciousness of America. As a colleague and friend, I applaud his efforts through the Illinois Fatherhood Initiative, the 21st Century Dads project and the Dads Honor Ride."

—Ken Canfield, PhD
Founder, National Center for Fathering

"No one is as dedicated toward, and as passionate about, this issue as David Hirsch. 21st Century Dads is a must read for everyone, it will provide you with insight to this issue that impacts all of us."

—Phil Cline, Chicago Police Memorial Foundation
Former Superintendent, Chicago Police Department

"Without responsible fathers in our world there will not be responsible children, or responsible citizens in the future. Efforts by David Hirsch's project 21CD are not only a very interesting initiative, but worth attention and support."

—Dr. Dariusz Cupiał, founder Tato.net
Lodz, Poland

"David Hirsch lives his life and passion on a daily basis. Through this book, he examines the role fathers have in our society and why their absence continues in the 21st century. He shares his passion to change this trajectory and thus change the world! Kudos to David for tackling head on a tough issue . . . and for living his life out loud!"

—Lisa M. Dietlin, President and CEO
The Institute of Transformational Philanthropy (ITP)

"'Walk lightly but carry a big stick' was advice given to me when I was a lad and to be honest I didn't have any idea what it meant. I met David Hirsch many years ago and saw what it meant in spades. 'Walk lightly.' He's quiet, soft-spoken, unassuming and old school polite. 'Carry a big stick.' He's a hard-working, compassionate, dedicated, confident, charitable man of his word. He's a true leader and I would follow him anywhere and especially on his journey to 'Break the Cycle of Father Absence.'"

—Tom Dreesen, entertainer

"David's story is personal but awakens and informs us all. His life has been devoted to powerful change and impact. Blood, sweat and tears, paired with ever mindful thought and meaningful collaboration, can't help but inspire. An extraordinary man, father and role model has finally documented his extraordinary journey."

—Kimberly T. Duchossois
The Duchossois Family Foundation

"David's personal story provides a compelling backdrop in defining his captivating life journey. The thoughtfulness with which he approaches the influences of family in general, and fathers in particular, serve as a call to order for everyone from fathers and father-figures, to leaders in our educational and political institutions. We all owe David a debt of gratitude for raising awareness and taking action in this impactful area."

—Chas Edelstein, Senior Advisor and Retired Co-CEO
Apollo Education Group, Inc.

"As a father of two and grandfather of five, I know firsthand the joys of fathering and the challenges too many families face when fathers are not present. I applaud David's effort to draw attention to the urgent need to encourage greater father involvement."

—Jim Edgar, former Governor of Illinois

"A moving, deeply engaging story that will inspire you to hug your kids, tell them you love them, and dive in harder than ever to the greatest job a man can ever have—fatherhood."

—Jonathan Eig, *New York Times* best-selling author, *Luckiest Man*

"David is particularly qualified to discuss the topic of fatherhood. Not as an academic or psychologist but as a Christian father. He speaks from the heart as a man who experienced a lonely soul as a child growing up without the love and guidance of a father in the home. His perspective on this serious problem in society is both internal and external. A unique view point."

—Daniel Genter, President
RNC Genter Capital Management

"David Hirsch's book is a fresh catalyst for communities, individuals and families to rethink, re-emphasize and re-imagine the role of fathers and fatherhood. The evolution of gender roles, the changing nature of family and the needs of children make this a timely, important contribution to the national dialogue on dads."

—Joline Godfrey, author, *Raising Financially Fit Kids*

"Having cycled across the country more than 85 times, including Route 66 dozens of times, I know firsthand the challenges David encountered. Riding 100+ miles a day for three weeks takes a level of commitment and perseverance few possess. I admire his Dads Honor Ride accomplishment and more importantly, the commitment he brings to bridging the gap for those growing up without dads."

—Lon Haldeman, Ultramarathon Cyclist, eight-time transcontinental record holder, and PAC Tour co-owner

"David Hirsch continues to bring his indispensable message of the role dads play in the 21st Century. It spells bright future, and we are grateful that David changes lives!"

—Frances Hesselbein, President and CEO
The Frances Hesselbein Leadership Institute

"Whether it was in his role as founder of the Illinois Fatherhood Initiative or as a father himself of five great children, David understands the critical importance of the role fathers play in the lives of the young. The journeys he has taken and shares in this book, both as a community leader and on his bicycle across America, offer pertinent lessons about the rich experiences that dads can provide to their kids when they are involved. Fathers from all backgrounds will find great comfort in the simple wisdom David provides in this outstanding read. Bravo!"

—David D. Hiller, President and CEO
Robert R. McCormick Foundation

"David Hirsch's extraordinary work through the Illinois Fatherhood Initiative has led to our awakening about the tragedy of absent fathers in the lives of America's children. The creative, determined work of The Initiative has proven that we can reverse the magnitude of this societal crisis by helping men re-establish healthy connections with their children. It simply takes enormous will, commitment and intelligent action to make real progress.

"David Hirsch exemplifies these human assets. The Dad's Honor Ride taken by committed citizens throughout the country is a brilliant and effective way to mobilize awareness of fatherhood absence, garner resources and celebrate the men who are now back in the game of developing their children. The boldness of the Honor Ride is an inspirational call to action to save the soul of our country. We ignore the call at our peril."

—Hubie Jones, Dean Emeritus, Boston University School of Social Work
Founder, Massachusetts Advocates for Children, Inc.

"David Hirsch has filled a void with this book and his Fatherhood Initiative. So many children need a father or father figure in their lives and David recognized the need to fill that void. I lost my father four years ago and miss that father figure in my life, sharing the good times and bad times. He was my role model who helped me to be the best father to my children. His work ethic was tireless and I strive to be the best from watching him firsthand. Every child needs that role model, friend, mentor and coach. Thank you, David, for writing this book and bringing the right message to the world about the value of a father or father figure in a child's life."

—Larry Kaufman, AVP Arthur J. Gallagher
Father to two incredible children

"David Hirsch knows firsthand the importance of fathers and father figures in the lives of children. He is a national leader in encouraging men to take an active role in making a positive impact in their children's lives. This call to action for men can make our world a better place—If we would listen and act upon it."

—Alan Krashesky, Broadcast Journalist

"There are many lessons to learn about being a father. Most of the time we have to learn these lessons on our own. David has written a simple guidebook about fatherhood to help fathers and grandfathers become better examples for their children and grandchildren."

—Allen J. Lynch, Medal of Honor recipient

"I was just barely into my 20s when I lost my own father, and for the past 40 plus years I have been forever grateful that I had his love, wisdom and guidance during my childhood. David Hirsch has tapped into just how important a father is to the family structure, and I applaud his insight into that aspect of our society."

—Joe Mantegna, actor, *Criminal Minds*

"I first met David more than two decades ago when he became a 1993 participant in the Kellogg National Fellowship Program. In an informal conversation, he shared his growing concern for the ineffectiveness of many men in their privileged role of fatherhood. In consequence, he launched the Illinois Fatherhood Initiative 19 years ago. Now, based on 26 years of personal experience as a father for his family and nearly two decades as an advocate for greater father involvement, he has written a book *21ˢᵗ Century Dads: A Father's Journey to Break the Cycle of Father Absence*. Whatever your role in parenthood (man or woman) I guarantee you will find this book of value!"

—Russell G. Mawby, Chair Emeritus
W. K. Kellogg Foundation

"Life doesn't always turn out like you planned. Being a father has been a challenge. I owe a debt of thanks to David Hirsch for helping me understand, no matter what the circumstances, we need to do everything we can to be present in the lives of our kids. I'm not able to do all the things I envisioned with my beautiful daughter Maggie, but I can demonstrate by my example to make the most of every day and that life is a gift. This book is an inspiration to all men who aspire to be the best dad they can be. Thank you for sharing your Dads Honor Ride experience."

—Jim Mullen, entrepreneur & disabled Chicago Police Officer

On October 17, 1996 Jim was catastrophically injured in the line of duty and became a quadriplegic. His daughter Maggie was 7 months at the time

"There's a lot of talk these days about fathers and the crisis of fatherlessness. David Hirsch doesn't just talk. He takes action. In Illinois, he envisioned and launched a statewide organization dedicated to encouraging and empowering dads. Nationally, he has shone a light on a problem that needs all our attention. With this book, he delivers practical insight for anyone who cares about the future of America. I dare you to take this ride."

—Jay Payleitner, national speaker and best-selling author,
52 Things Kids Need from a Dad and *The Dad Manifesto*

"David Hirsch not only models what being a good father looks like, he helps the rest of us get better, too."

—Eboo Patel, Founder and President,
Interfaith Youth Core

"Today's modern thinking has brought confusion and less tolerance for families and specifically the need and roles of fathers. In recent years, programs available to families in Native American communities have focused primarily on the needs of women and children. Today, Native American men are often viewed as the cause of many family and social problems in their communities. NAFFA takes the position that fathers are:

- The solution to addressing the problems.
- The greatest untapped resource
- Fathers must take the lead in keeping families together

"The family is at the heart of Native American cultures. I have had the opportunity to meet and share thoughts with David. We continue to support and appreciate his ongoing commitment to fatherhood and the importance of families. Thank you for all the efforts, David!'

—Albert M Pooley, President/Founder
Native American Fatherhood & Families Association (NAFFA)

"As a father of three wonderful children, I understand the importance of guiding each child in life decisions. Having the guidance of a father, or father figure is absolutely life changing. Illinois Fatherhood initiative and 21st Century Dads Foundation gives hope and chances to those in need of that exact thing. Thank you, David, for caring just that extra bit."

—Tony Schumacher, eight-time NHRA National Champion
Top Fuel Pilot U.S. Army Drag Racing Team

"Growing up without a father in the home after age 12, it has been a life-long passion of mine to help facilitate healthy, thriving families. David Hirsch shares the same passion, and has devoted the last 20 years to recognizing and applauding men of character who have chosen to lead by example and be the pillars of their homes and communities. He is a devoted husband and father with a love of adventure, and passed that love down to his five children who are now young, successful adults; precisely what Fatherhood is all about."

—Mike Singletary, former Chicago Bear/NFL Hall of Fame

"My friend David Hirsch has written an excellent book for us 21st Century Dads. It's funny how this role, the most important job we will ever have, comes with no 'owner's manual' or 'training tips.' But David helps fill the gap with an inspirational telling of his own fatherhood journey, all through the lens of the Dad's Honor Ride to help bring attention to the epidemic of fatherhood absence, which is destroying our inner cities and many other communities across the U.S.

My congratulations to David for a great book as well as my sincere thanks for his passion for fatherhood and zeal for life. You're going to enjoy this book!!"

—Gregory W. Slayton

The Honorable Gregory W. Slayton is the author of the global best-seller Be a Better Dad Today *which has sold over 250,000 copies in 25+ countries since its publication in 2012. Slayton is also a venture capitalist and a man of faith who has raised four great kids with his wife of 26 years.*

"David Hirsch addresses one of society's greatest challenges—the systemic disengagement of fathers. Children without an engaged and present father represents one of the most highly-disadvantaged demographic groups in the nation. The physical and emotional absence of a father in a child's life often translates into that child's own emotional unavailability; children can find it difficult or nearly impossible to envision and embrace achieving success in school and life. Thanks to David Hirsch for opening this urgent dialogue and helping us to pursue every opportunity to support our children, encourage their father's involvement whenever possible, and find positive male role models to help us guide our children's lives."

—Lisa Stamos, President
Quintessential Media Group, Inc.

"I was there from start to finish, all 2,300+ miles, as a crew member. The Dads Honor Ride was a transformative experience. To do something like this requires more than training and skills. It requires "Heart" and the "Drive" to make things happen. A natural outcome is this book by David Hirsch, who has the Skills, the Drive and the Heart! Fatherhood has a wonderful champion whose story is captured beautifully between these covers!!!"

—O. Lawton "Wilk" Wilkerson, Original Tuskegee Airman

"Being a 21ˢᵗ Century father takes courage and strength. Not the physical and life daring type but courage and strength through character and commitment to our families. Fathers of all ages and backgrounds can pull wisdom from the best practices and inspirational stories David has compiled. A true must read."

—Shawn H. Wilson, Ford Motor Company Fund

21st Century Dads

A Father's Journey to Break
the Cycle of Father Absence

David A. Hirsch

with John St. Augustine

Transformation Media Books
Bloomington, Indiana

Published by Transformation Media Books, USA

Transformation Media Books

www.TransformationMediaBooks.com
info@TransformationMediaBooks.com

An imprint of Pen & Publish, Inc.
www.PenandPublish.com
Bloomington, Indiana
(314) 827-6567

Print ISBN: **978-1-941799-35-2**
eBook ISBN: **978-1-941799-36-9**

21CD Logo and Cover Image:
Maureen Roberts, Signature Graphic Design

Cover Design: Jennifer Geist

Bell Curve image by Mwtoews [CC BY 2.5], via Wikimedia Commons

3 6109 00509 5283

To Peggy, who makes me a better father
To my grandfathers, Sam Solomon & Harry Hirsch
To my mom, Claire, my dad, Ralph & my brother, Ron
To my extraordinary children: Dave, Amanda, Emily, Charlie & Addie
To all fathers & father-figures who prioritize the interest in children

Table of Contents

Acknowledgments

To my friend Lisa Dieltin, who started the domino effect of new acquaintances who helped make this project possible, including: Jenniffer Weigel a gifted communicator, her friend John St. Augustine my kindred spirit, his long-time friend Ginny Weissman who somehow pulled the pieces of this puzzle together, and Jennifer Geist of Transformation Media Books for taking a flyer on a first time author. Also special thanks to long-time friends John Bellamy and Abe Thompson for the introduction to Emma Young.

On the fathering front, there have been so many men who have shaped my life, but especially: Dr. Ken Canfield, founder of the National Center for Fathering who has been a guiding light to me and countless other here and abroad. The late Peter Spokes whose death had a more profound impact on my life than the many gifts he provided during his life. My grandfathers: Sam Solomon, who was there every step of the way for me through my age 40 and his age 93 and Harry Hirsch, who immigrated from Nazi Germany in September 1939 and his emphasis on the importance of education being something no one can take away from you. All the men and women, businesses, and foundations who have supported the Illinois Fatherhood Initiative. Without you, there would be no IFI.

To the extraordinary group who came together to create and execute the Dads Honor Ride, which came to be in less than four months. Especially neighbor and uber biker friend Bob Lee, my role model for combining riding and fundraising. The legendary Lon Haldeman, for taking me under your wing and helping me in so many aspects of the ride. My good friend and neighbor Gary Grube (AKA: BIG Brother) for the use of your tricked out vehicle and all the safety equipment. Mark Stephan my functional quadriplegic friend who has proven anything is possible. Jim Mullen one of my other quadriplegic friends who I draw great strength from, especially when I'm bumping up against my limits. Tom Dreesen, who is like a father to me and for being there at the beginning and the end. My "old" friend, Lawton "Wilk" Wilkerson, one of the Original Tuskegee Airman, for being my wingman from start to finish on the DHR. Lincoln Baker my ride director and his super fit wife Courtney Riley, who set the pace the first four days. My fellow riders in order of appearance; Chris Miller, Shawn Taylor, Dave Hirsch, Patrick and Maciej Wierzchucki, Darek Cupial, Peggy Hirsch, Bob Lee and Jorge Solorio. The crew members not previously mentioned; Addie Hirsch and Jaroslaw Wiszowaty. My work colleagues James Kelly and Sara Keller who made it possible to be away from the office for three weeks. The primary sponsors: Motorola Solutions Foundation, Robert R. McCormick Foundation and The Duchossois Family Foundation. And last but not least, God for giving me the courage and faith that anything is possible with your partnership.

Foreword

My father was just short of his 70th birthday back in 2004. There I was at 45 with a family of my own and all the responsibilities in the world, watching over him like he did so many times in my life. A zillion thoughts raced through my mind, the big one being the concept of "the assembly line" that unseen, and too often unspoken, inevitable transition that takes place when a boy has to say goodbye to his father and then take his place next in line.

The sun was shining that May morning when my father took his last breath. I had stayed with him the night before he died, putting cool towels on his forehead to help stave off the fever that came with the final hours of his life. There was no one else in the room besides the two of us, stark walls illuminated by the glowing lights of the monitors and a constant chorus of "beeps" that came and went, his vital signs displayed on the little screens. To be with him when he took his last breath, as he was with me when I took my first, was an honor beyond words.

I was fortunate to have his presence in my life. The good and the bad all taught me lessons that were disguised as problems and difficulties, hard work and challenging conversations, as two generations attempted to understand each other as best we could. His advice to me over the years was short to the point and profound, "The best investment you can make is in your talents and time. That way you will always know who you are and what you stand for."

It's those words that remind me of David Hirsch.

I knew a bit about the Illinois Fatherhood Initiative, hearing bits and pieces about their efforts over the years, but it wasn't until I met David at lunch through our mutual friend Jenniffer Weigel that I made the connection he was the guy behind it all. In between visits to the buffet table, I listened to him talk about his life, his wife and children, his father and grandfather. He shared with a deep conviction that only comes from experience about his "Dads Honor Ride" that encompassed a journey across the western United States on a bicycle seat for over 2,300 miles. He leaned forward a bit in his chair when he talked about how important it was for him to get the word out regarding one of the greatest challenges facing our society today, the gaping wound of "father absence." Here was this fairly mild- mannered fellow, a bit soft spoken at first, becoming more and more intense as the lunch went on. All of that inner drive and energy that he used to push past his personal and professional barriers while pedaling countless hours, was focused on behalf of children that he would never meet, those statistics that make the headlines, so many of which are the byproduct of not having a father in their lives. I was struck by his sincerity and intent, both of which are a very rare thing in the world today.

By the time lunch was over, I was ready to get on a bike next to him, thankfully for those of us not used to riding 100 miles a day, this book is the next best thing. *21ˢᵗ Century Dads* is not only a virtual ride along with David and his team of superheroes filled with snapshots that take you off the beaten path, past the headlines to meet some incredible men making a serious difference for those kids without a dad, but it's also a guidepost for becoming a better father. As you look over David's shoulder as he comes upon the "Trail of Tears," you begin to understand when you break the chains of the past, it sets your children free in the future. This book can help you do just that whether you are an absent dad or with your children in a traditional family. Each chapter is filled with insights and inspiration that only comes from the place where rubber meets the road, conversations and conversions along famed Route 66, and one man's insistence that many of the ills of our society can be cured when a father takes his rightful place in his child's life.

David completed his incredible journey in just 21 days, however the ripple effect of his efforts is still creating serious waves when it comes to the ongoing impact we can make as fathers in the lives our children. The lasting legacy this book promises is well worth the ride.

John St. Augustine
Award-winning talk radio host
Author, *Living An Uncommon Life* and *Every Moment Matters*

Prologue

What would your reaction be if someone, who you've known for less than 30 minutes, tells you your highly dysfunctional relationship with your father was a *gift*? My first reaction was this guy has absolutely no (*insert your favorite curse word here and fill in the blank*) idea of what he's talking about.

That is what happened when I first met talk radio host, author and speaker John St. Augustine, just four months ago. There we were sitting down to lunch in the dining room of the Union League Club of Chicago. To compound the situation, he's the guest of Jenn Weigel, a mutual friend.

I'm thinking, *The nerve of this guy.*

My actual response was: "John, with all due respect you have no idea what you're talking about. A gift is something that comes with a bow on it. The psychological slippery slope I've been on the past 49 years bears no resemblance to any gift. Plus, gifts are things you look forward to, things you ask for, things others do to please you. Let's be real."

John's response was more than illuminating. "Hey, I know we've just met, but it's clear to me, even in this brief conversation, you have an extraordinary passion for your wife and kids. You've also dedicated the better part of 20 years to drawing attention to the importance of father involvement. And, you've had an immeasurable impact on people here in Illinois, across the country and beyond. Whether you realize it or not, you're the man you are, the husband you are, and the father you are, all as a result of that messed up relationship with your dad."

Spiritual 2x4 whack over my head, right there at the table while I was eating a salad.

It took my Neanderthal brain a couple of extra moments to process what I just heard. Then *pop* the light bulb goes on and grows brighter and brighter. It was one of life's "aha" moments when your perspective shifts and you see yourself or your situation in a new light. Everything seems a little clearer, like you've put on a pair of glasses you didn't think you needed. It was a liberating experience and one that has led to a growing friendship.

Thank you, John, for helping me develop a better understanding of my situation. It's with that conversation (and others) in mind that I offer you this book.

Actually, the idea for this book has been with me since I finished the "21st Century Dads Honor Ride 2015" that took me far out of my comfort zone. After 2,300+ miles in 21 days, I had no choice but to grow into a much better version of David Hirsch than the guy who stood in the kitchen and told my wife Peggy that I was going ride halfway across the country to bring awareness to the challenges of fatherhood and the devastating effects of father absence.

As 21st Century Dads, we need to be there for our kids in what I call *The Quadrant* or the four essential ingredients of being a father. The goal is to stem the tide for 24 million kids who are in danger of never finding out who they are and, more importantly, who they can be in order to lead healthy, productive lives.

Those four pillars of fatherhood are really very simple. As fathers we absolutely need to be present; *financially*, *physically*, *emotionally* and *spiritually*, and that order is always changing according to current conditions. What your son needs from you at six, is different than what he needs at 13, but the foundation that comes from the early years is essential in creating a lifelong relationship that is always challenging, often in flux and at times frustrating.

But just like this journey I am on, it's worth every mile.

If we as fathers are to make a positive impact on our children, we must first and foremost be diligent in working on ourselves. You cannot give something to someone else that you don't already have. And if you grew up, as I did, without *The Quadrant* then it's on you to let go of what was, accept what is and begin your own *Honor Ride* towards creating that positive ripple effect of change. In the back of this book you can find resources that will help you build your own foundation as a father and in doing so ensure your children and grandchildren never have to question your love, commitment and faith in them.

Riding a bike halfway across the country has been miraculous on many levels. The people I have met, the lessons I learned and the things I discovered in myself have helped me become a better father, husband *and* human being. Every day when I got back on the bike to begin another leg of the journey, I came across some incredible people, places and events that taught me great lessons, restored my faith and shed light onto my path. I also found that each of these moments included in this book (and many more that are not) in some way, shape or form was a teaching or lesson in fatherhood. It was as if a "divine assignment" of sorts was in the making and while much attention was given to the effort I was putting in by pedaling, truly the foundation of the ride became these amazing incidents and synchronicity of coincidences that at times left me in tears, other times with chills and always a smile, hug or handshake.

Truly, the more empowered you are as a man and as a dad, the greater chance your children have of leading lives of substance and significance on so many levels.

So this is a call to action. I invite you along on this "honor ride," and my hope is you not only enjoy the moments and messages from this journey but also that you garner *inspiration*, along with some *information* that can lead to *transformation* when it comes to those very important three letters.

Dad.

Okay, let's take a ride.

Dads Honor Ride is a cycling and fundraising campaign. The inaugural ride, DHR15, took place from June 1–21, 2015.

The ride started in Santa Monica, California, loosely followed the iconic Route 66 and concluded in Chicago, Illinois, on Father's Day at U.S. Cellular Field with an on-field ceremony before the Chicago White Sox baseball game.

Here is the route day by day with actual mileage*

Day 1 - Santa Monica to Palm Springs, CA (149 miles)
Day 2 - Palm Springs to Blythe, CA (130 miles)
Day 3 - Blythe, CA to Wickenburg, AZ (114 miles)
Day 4 - Wickenburg to Cottonwood, AZ (111 miles)
Day 5 - Cottonwood to Winslow, AZ (94 miles)
Day 6 - Winslow to Gallup, NM (140 miles)
Day 7 - Gallup to Albuquerque, NM (141 miles)
Day 8 - Albuquerque to Santa Rosa, NM (94 miles)
Day 9 - Santa Rosa to Tucumcari, NM (110 miles)
Day 10 - Tucumcari to Amarillo, TX (110 miles)
Day 11 - Amarillo to Shamrock, TX (102 miles)
Day 12 - Shamrock to Weatherford, OK (102 miles)
Day 13 - Weatherford to Chandler, OK (100 miles)
Day 14 - Chandler to Claremore, OK (92 miles)
Day 15 - Claremore to Joplin, MO (103 miles)
Day 16 - Joplin to Lebanon, MO (127 miles)
Day 17 - Lebanon to Sullivan, MO (94 miles)
Day 18 - Sullivan to Edwardsville, IL (94 miles)
Day 19 - Edwardsville to Lincoln, IL (122 miles)
Day 20 - Lincoln to Monee, IL (151 miles)
Day 21 - Monee to Chicago, IL (37 miles)

*actual mileage recorded on the Map My Ride App.

One
The Father Factor

It is much easier to become a father than to be one.

—Kent Nerburn

It's day four of the Dads Honor Ride, and I am perched on the seat of my bike, somewhere in Arizona between Flagstaff and Winslow, sloshing through a constant downpour. I have ridden over 500 miles the first four days which has me looking forward to taking a breather "on a corner in Winslow" like the song says. Except I have many miles to go before that happens. My legs are still strong and, as I have come to know, more than anything else, this is quickly becoming a mind over matter deal.

But I can't take it easy. Not just yet.

This ride, however, is all about finding a place to make a stand or in my case . . . *a ride* . . . on a bicycle from Santa Monica, California, to Chicago, Illinois, a distance of 2,300+ miles in just twenty-one days.

Prior to training for this ride, I had only done one century ride (100 miles in a day) and that was in September of 2009. This trip isn't about getting ready for some race or even a mid-life crisis. It's about something far more important.

I know what you are thinking.

What is it that makes a 54-year-old father of five take three weeks off work, push aside my duties at home and cross the western United States on a bicycle? Why would I put myself in this position, push myself like never before and stretch my limits in such a way?

The answer is really very simple: It's about being a *Dad*.

In many ways, this "Dads Honor Ride" is an extension of the work I started 19 years earlier when I founded Illinois Fatherhood Initiative (IFI) back in 1997. IFI is the country's first state-wide nonprofit fatherhood organization whose mission is "Connecting Children and Fathers." IFI is another of my resources that, as a social entrepreneur, has had a definitive impact on what I think is one of the most serious challenges facing America in the 21st century. *Father Absence.*

1

Research shows that children who grow up without their fathers have: lower high school graduation rates, are more likely to be involved with gangs and crimes, abuse alcohol and drugs, often become teen parents, may suffer from depression and commit suicide and frequently become incarcerated. When a father abandons his responsibilities, children suffer, the mothers of the children suffer, and society at-large suffers. *That* is why I am on a bike in the middle of Arizona drenched from head to toe, getting sprayed by the whoosh of semi-trailers, head down trying to avoid debris and making sure to avoid potholes disguised as puddles, wearing a cycling jersey with "21st Century Dads Honor Ride" emblazoned across my chest.

As I push on, there is more that drives me to complete the journey. My goal is to bring awareness to the vitally important role fathers occupy in the lives of their children because I know firsthand what it feels like when that rudder, influence and presence are not there. It's a vast empty feeling as if a part of my soul was missing. The part that stands for something larger than life, a spirit, if you will, of the male energy of a father and the connection that can make or break a child's life, and how they see themselves in the world.

I was six when my parents divorced.

The sting of that time still lingers and I think it's one of the reasons I feel so blessed to have been married to my wife and best friend Peggy for 33 years. At times, Peggy has reminded me when I was spending too much time inspiring other dads to be part of their child's life, that *our* five children also needed their dad.

"Hey 'Mr. Fatherhood,' you are all fired up about making sure kids stay connected to their dads, how about walking your talk and spending some time with ours?" she would say.

Shot across the bow, message received, course correction made.

Peggy's words, in and of themselves, offer a lesson not only in crystal clear communication but also a commitment that needs to be in place in a relationship involving children, whether you are married or not. Can't get on the stump (or bike) and ring the proverbial bell about the dangers of being an absent father, and then become one myself!

While Peggy is always there to help me put my rudder back in place towards hearth and home, deep inside me that six-year-old boy is still very adamant about the message of fatherhood absence, because my feelings from childhood are burned into my being.

From age six to 13, I had very little contact with my father. I didn't understand why my dad moved away, remarried and became a dad to someone else's kids. Then in a strange twist of fate, I ended up living with my dad at 13 and I had the chance, up close, to have experiences that would forever change my perceptions of family and fatherhood.

The experience would solidify my firm belief you can learn just as much, or more, from good as well bad role models.

My dad and his parents came over from Germany when he was eight, in September of 1939, just as Poland was being invaded starting WWII. They spoke no English at home and life was hard growing up. As he got older, I think he took to the notion of America being the land of opportunity and identified in some ways as a Hugh Hefner-type character. Nothing like being an impressionable young man and trying to figure out why your dad wears shirts with the first four to five buttons unbuttoned exposing gold chains. Let's just say his sense of priorities and what he valued was more about him and maintaining an image than about family. It was a deep contrast to his father who emphasized the value of knowledge. Grandpa Hirsch, having lost most everything, would often proclaim, "education is most important, since it's something that can't be taken away from you."

The pain was already very deep in me then and living with my father and stepmother drove it in even more. The lessons I learned from them and how they parented would, in many ways, provide the foundation for being a much better father to my own children. It has also influenced all the work I do in raising awareness of the serious negative ripple effect of absent fathers, even when they live under the same roof as their children.

The biggest lesson my dad gave me, and the one that can literally make or break your relationship with your kids, is really very easy but something I found out the hard way.

I was off to college at the University of Illinois. My parents although divorced agreed to split paying my tuition. My mom paid her half from her modest savings and earnings as a Chicago Public School teacher. I would take out student loans to be paid back by my father with the understanding I maintain a "B" average. I proudly graduated in four years with a degree in accounting, a highly sought after job at Price Waterhouse (one of the BIG eight) after being super involved in extracurricular affairs, including serving as president of my local fraternity and serving on the national board for Theta Xi. When I received my diploma my GPA was 3.9 just a bit shy of 4.0 out of a 5.0 scale. Mission accomplished or so I thought.

"Well son, it looks like you came up a little short," he said wiggling out of our agreement. While it's true I had a B average, but not a 4.0, there was no discussion of common ground regarding his end of the deal and that . . . was that. That decision not to honor our agreement would have a devastating impact on our relationship for the next decade and beyond.

So, every month for the next 10 years, I found a way to come up with $87.29 until the loans were paid off. That was a lesson in itself, noted and filed away, for other times when I needed a reminder of fiscal discipline. But the bigger lesson came at the end of a decade, a very difficult 10 years that had my father and I growing further and further apart over *$87.29/month*. The cost of which, measured in terms of our relationship, was far greater. That lack of connection and communication was compound interest of the worst kind.

For 10 years it burned a hole right through me.

Toward the end of those 10 years, Peggy asked what I was going to do once I had paid off the loans?

"I am just going to tell him I paid off my student loans," I said, not really looking forward to the conversation but I felt he needed to know I had taken care of the obligation. When I finally did tell him about 10 years of payments, figuring out how to meet my obligations, then as a father of two young kids always making sure I paid on time. He looked at me with a blank face.

"I don't know what you are talking about . . ." he said.

I was stunned in some ways but not surprised. That is when the first and foremost lesson of being a "21ˢᵗ Century Dad" was put in place.

The importance of keeping your word.

Communication builds bridges. Miscommunication burns them down and over time they get harder and harder to build back up. It's been said that those who push our buttons the most usually teach us the most. My father was a great teacher to me. When I finally stood back and took in all the information on his life, removing myself from the victim chair and realizing, had he been different, I would have been different. Everything started to shift in me. Anger was being replaced by understanding, pain lessened and purpose began to form. Fear gave way to a deep faith and, mostly importantly, every mile I put behind me healed a part of my past and opened up new roads for the future.

While I couldn't do anything about the gold chains my dad wore on his chest, I could do something about breaking the chains of a father's absence in the lives of my children and for others. That hole burning in me began to close, to heal and to fill with something other than anger. It took me a long while to forgive my father for not being who I thought he should be, which then gave me permission to become who I could be.

So there I was, a 54-year-old father of five on a bike, with moderate (at best) athletic ability, pedaling his way to Winslow, Arizona, with a couple of thousand miles ahead of me.

Pretty cool.

Two

Father's Day

Honor your father and your mother, so that you may
live for a long time in the land the LORD your God is giving you.
—Exodus 20:12

Dads Honor Ride 2015 was an extraordinary 2,300+ mile journey from Santa Monica, California, to Chicago, Illinois. There was much coordination and planning to have me arrive on Father's Day to address the congregation at Progressive Baptist Church and then at an on-field presentation before the Chicago White Sox Father's Day baseball game.

Truth be told my first Father's Day falls on September 15, the second one is March 5, the third is July 27, the fourth (wait there's more) is May 31 and ta-da . . . my fifth Father's Day is October 18. These are my children's birthdays so five times a year I celebrate Father's Day, along with the traditional "buy dad a tie, a mug or make the obligatory call" national holiday celebrated the third Sunday in June. While the wind whistles through my helmet, and I squint into the midday sun, I often think about how all this started. Not my ride, so much (*I will get to that later*) but the actual holiday itself.

The very first observance of "Father's Day" was held on July 5, 1908 in Fairmont, West Virginia, just two months after Ann Jarvis held a celebration for her mother, who had passed away, in Grafton about 15 miles from Fairmont creating the first "Mother's Day." Grace Golden Clayton was mourning the loss of her father in December of 1907 when he died in a mining disaster in the nearby town of Monongah, along with 360 other men, 250 of them fathers, leaving behind thousands of fatherless children. Putting aside her own grief, Grace went to her pastor, Robert Thomas Webb, and suggested that a day should be set aside to honor the fathers who had died. This one time "honoring" was never promoted outside of Fairmont, but it is the foundation for all other future events.

One year later in 1909, Sonora Smart Dodd would hear a sermon, in the Central Methodist Episcopal Church in Spokane, about the Mother's

Day (and possibly Father's Day) celebrations held in West Virginia the year prior. Long before telephones, texting and Facebook, word of mouth carried the news of the day. The Fourth Commandment, "Honour thy father and thy mother," was the basis of the sermon.

Dodd thought of her own father, William Jackson Smart, who had raised six children as a single parent. Like Grace Golden Clayton just two years before her, Dodd went to her pastor and suggested an "honor ceremony" to be held on her father's birthday, June 5. After much discussion, it was agreed that several churches would celebrate "Father's Day" with a sermon, but they needed time to prepare their words, and the third Sunday of June 19, 1910 is recognized as the first time that a public display by a group of people in one city honored fathers.

It's interesting to note that after just a few years, "Father's Day" sermons fell into relative obscurity. By 1920, Dodd had stopped promoting the idea as she would go on to study at the famed Art Institute of Chicago but 10 years later in 1930, she returned to Spokane, and stoked the fires of fatherhood once again. Around all this activity, a bill was introduced in 1913 to make "Father's Day" a national holiday and in 1916, President Woodrow Wilson went to Spokane to speak at a Father's Day celebration and wanted to make it official, but Congress resisted, fearing that it would become commercialized.

Imagine that, the Congress of The United States of America not wanting to grant a holiday because retailers might take advantage of it.

Two more failed attempts to have a bill passed failed and in 1957 it was U.S. Senator Margaret Chase Smith from Maine, who wrote a proposal accusing Congress of ignoring fathers for 40 years while honoring mothers, thus "[singling] out just one of our two parents."

Wow, first the concern about retailers and now Congress "ignoring the role of fathers."

Huh?

Still nothing . . . and it wasn't until 1966, as the Viet Nam war began to escalate, taking fathers away from their homes to fight in the jungles of Southeast Asia, did President Lyndon Baines Johnson issue the first presidential proclamation honoring fathers, designating the third Sunday in June as Father's Day. The day was made a permanent national holiday six years later when President Richard Nixon signed it into law in 1972.

For the most part, Americans have never fully embraced the celebration of "Dad" viewing it as nothing more than an opportunity for retailers to piggyback off the commercial success of "Mother's Day." It was actually Sonora Smart Dodd who had approached many trade groups who represented merchandise that would have the most to gain from a holiday, manufacturers of pipes, tobacco and, of course . . . ties.

So why all this historical background information?

Because it's important to understand history, the root cause of any movement, especially something as important as fatherhood. A woman who was grieving the loss of her father, 109 years ago, was so moved by the deaths of hundreds of men, young and old, fathers of all ages in a mining disaster, that she took action to honor them. Twenty-four months later, the words of a sermon brought Sonora Smart Dodd to tears, thinking about her own father, Civil War veteran and single parent . . . raising six kids on his own, (in very different times than now) and she also takes action. The ripple effect of love, these two women had for the role and importance of fatherhood, led to countless hours of dedication and admiration for fathers and finally, 60+ years later, a national holiday to honor them.

With all that in mind I use the third Sunday in June as my *inspiration destination* all the while knowing each of our respective Father's Days is first and foremost celebrated the moment your child is born, that instant you hold a new life in your arms, the very essence of hope itself, manifest in your son or daughter. It's the day you transitioned from being just a man to also being a father. From that point on, fathering is a role in flux, depending on the needs of your child, from changing diapers, to the their first words, to their first tooth and on through first steps and all that follows. Skinned knees and elbows, broken bones and broken hearts, late nights and early mornings, locked doors and open windows and a thousand other opportunities that are built in to being called "Dad."

There is much I have learned as the father of five.

You will never have ALL your ducks in a row and, most days especially early on, you will feel like you are stumbling through the experience of "dad" as each day is truly a new day. If all you do is repeat how you were parented growing up, no matter how it was, then you are simply recreating the past instead of affecting the future.

And being a dad, especially in the 21st century, is all about affecting the future, as your children become the imprint of your presence on levels seen and unseen. If you attended birthing classes, you learned about the process of your child coming into the world, but after the day your son or daughter arrives is when the real lessons begin, and only end when you do.

It takes a deep desire to apply "conscious" fathering as opposed to the old "do as I say and not as I do" philosophy so many grew up with. Being a 21ˢᵗ century dad entails not just putting in time but also making time. It's not just about paying bills but paying attention. It's more than being a steady presence but also being fully present. More than ever before it's not trying to be "the man of steel" but rather "a man who is real" with shortcomings, faults and mistakes. Not being an idol but rather an approachable and attainable "ideal" of fatherhood that is somewhere between "Father Knows Best" and "My Three Sons" or in my case, "My Three Daughters & Two Sons."

This Dads Honor Ride was an effort to raise awareness for the vital role of the father as part of the blueprint put in place by two incredible women over one hundred years ago. Back then life, of course, was very different.

The average life expectancy was 47, most workers earned $200 to $400 per year, and most Americans had no real concept of "airplanes."

So while it might be tough as a single parent now, imagine the obstacles and challenges Dodd's father must have encountered when there were only 45 stars on the flag. He became a widower when his wife died giving birth to their sixth child at home, where 95% of children were born back then.

Tough stuff to say the least. But something inside him *knew* he could rise above and carry on, making such an impact on his daughter that she lobbied to have the first "Father's Day" on his birthday.

Ah . . . that *knowing*.

One of the most important traits you can develop as a dad, is a "knowing." That is, in part, a byproduct of your life experiences but also a growing sense of faith that as challenging, difficult, scary and confusing as fatherhood can be at times, there is a deep well within your heart that just "knows." That only comes with experience, *but sometimes* you have to have the "knowing first" and no more prominent was that lesson than the night before leaving for LA, to begin the first "Dads Honor Ride." After spending the better part of four months (February to May) contemplating all aspects of the ride and putting in approximately 1,800 training miles during April and May, my wife said to me, "How do you know you're going to be able to ride 100+ miles a day, for 21 days, with no days off?"

After acknowledging I didn't know I was capable of doing this—even though during my training I had done eight century rides, including three sets of two back to back—I simply remarked "I'm not sure, but if I don't try, I'll never know."

Whether you are a single dad like Sergeant William Jackson Smart from the Union's First Arkansas Light Artillery during the Civil War or a guy like me with a college degree, years of business acumen and the father of five, it is incumbent on us to absolutely become the best role model our children will ever have. The indelible mark made on them by us either becomes a bridge for them to become great role models for their own children, (your grandchildren) or barriers to the possibilities that are abundant in changing the future by raising whole, aware vibrant fathers (and mothers) who much like our heroines, Grace Golden Clayton and Sonora Smart Dodd, made sure that "Father's Day" is not forgotten.

Plus, you might get some really great ties.

It might be very difficult to "honor thy father and thy mother" depending on the circumstances you grew up in. I know firsthand how hard that can be as I have struggled with the relationship with my own father over the years, but while you cannot change the past, you can change the future. There is great power in *knowing* that opportunity exists for you in this very moment.

Part of that *for me* was riding a bicycle a couple of thousand miles from the west coast to the shores of Lake Michigan, *for you* it might be simply knocking off work early and surprising your kid at a game or event or turning off the television and talking with (*not to*) your child. Become immersed in their lives, not to the point of being a "helicopter parent" hovering over every move, but just enough so that later in life, when they need to talk *with you*, that bridge will be there.

Father's Day starts the day your child is born and, in actuality . . . is *every* day.

Three
Your Own Pace

My father used to play with my brother and me in the yard.
Mother would come out and say, "You're tearing up the grass."
"We're not raising grass," my dad would reply, "we're raising boys."
—Harmon Killebrew

When we first left Santa Monica on June 1, 2015, there were three riders: myself; Courtney Riley, a friend from Evanston who is a super-fit yoga instructor and Ironman triathlete; and an acquaintance of my Ride Director Lincoln Baker, Chris Miller from St. Louis. Chris is the father of two young kids and a U.S. Army veteran that had served two tours in Afghanistan. They are both in their late 30s and were committed to ride for the first few days before heading home.

While I was very thankful for their involvement and companionship it became evident we had different skill levels and different time frames. While we rode together a good portion of the 149 miles to Palm Springs, Chris struggled to keep up since he had not adequately prepared, which meant he spent some time riding in the support vehicles part of the day. It was just the opposite with Courtney. I felt like I was holding her back so, periodically, I'd say, "Keep going at your pace, I'll catch up to you."

With Addie on Santa Monica Pier minutes before embarking on the 2,300+ mile ,21-day journey.

I was highly focused on maintaining a pace I was comfortable with and not expending any more energy than necessary. This was a ride and not a race, and I was certainly not going to let my male ego get bruised by a female companion. We only had to stop once for mechanical purposes the first day, to change a flat tire on Courtney's bike. Based on the Map My Ride app that we used to track our mileage every day, we maintained a respectable 15 mph pace over the 149 miles logged that day. And what a long day it was as we arrived in Palm Springs with headlamps on, in the dark of night around 9 p.m.

Being on the road from 7 a.m. to 9 p.m. the first day provided some good time to reflect, and this idea about riding at your own pace and not comparing yourself to others reminded me about some important lessons I learned in my mid-30s.

One very important experience took place in July 1995 while at the Gallup Leadership Institute in Lincoln, NE. I was one of 20 participants there for the week, including 12 of us Group 13 Fellows from W.K. Kellogg Foundation. We were there to learn about leadership and to undergo some very thorough examinations to determine what type of leaders we were and learn about our "drivers."

We had the pleasure of directly interacting with Donald O. Clifton, CEO of the Gallup Organization, who was in his early 70s. He was very deliberate about modeling the "Dipper & the Bucket Theory." The long and short of it is when your bucket is full you can accomplish anything. He preached that we each have the ability to add a drop to someone's bucket with a smile, a friendly hello, a note of thanks or praise or some positive affirmation. On the other hand, we can dip into someone's bucket, by making negative remarks in their presence or behind their back. Berating some in public when a private one-on-one conversation would have been more appropriate or simply not acknowledging someone's existence or contribution were other ways to help drain someone's bucket.

Don went as far as having note cards die cut in the shape of tear drops that he used to share little messages, "drops" of affirmation. Twenty-one years later, I still have one of those teardrop messages to serve as a tangible reminder of our encounter and his influence.

The main reason I got to thinking about Gallup and the July 1995 experience, had to do with the surprise finding their "20 Theme Analysis" discovered about me. After doing a very thorough analysis, including information from supervisors, peers and subordinates at work, reams of written exams and firsthand observations on site, their conclusion was that I was not driven by "competition."

My first response was 'then everyone who has ever met me the first 34 years of my life must be wrong.' I had been told forever how competitive I am. As the folks at Gallup explained it, people have "misdiagnosed you." Gallup's analysis revealed *what really drives you is* "achievement."

I said naively "I don't understand what you're talking about, could you explain this?"

The short explanation is, some people are "competitive." They have to win. Coming in second place is the equivalent of losing. It's a zero sum game and there can only be one winner. It's more of the sports model of winners and losers.

Those who are "achievement" oriented set goals for themselves and work very diligently to achieve their goals regardless of what others might be doing around them. Another important difference is those who are achievement oriented can celebrate other's success, not a trait always associated with competitive types.

It was one of those light bulb moments. It was actually a very liberating experience to know and be comfortable with doing things at own my pace and focus on what I set out to do.

Let's bring this back to why it's important to us as dads.

First takeaway: *We all have different drivers.* Know what moves you and be attune to what motivates your kids. Secondly, *set your own standards* for the dad you want to be. Most start with the level of their father and work up (*or down*) from there. But, what if you're like me and you didn't have that strong father role model? Then you have to develop your own standards, find your own "True North" and plot your own course.

There is a Father's Self-Assessment Tool included in the Resources in the back of this book for that purpose. It will provide you with some immediate feedback in four areas of *The Quadrant* (*financial, physical, emotional* and *spiritual*). If you're honest and objective with yourself, you'll be able to identify some areas for improvement.

Powerful learning experiences come in many forms. The only sport I really know something about is baseball. I played baseball from age five all the way through high school. As a dad, I coached 13 mostly youth travel baseball teams. We took the boys to tournaments in Cooperstown a couple of times, Omaha for the College World Series, Florida, Arizona and countless tournaments around the Midwest. My older son Dave played varsity baseball through high school. His younger brother, Charlie, who is a lefty pitcher, first baseman and centerfielder, was one of the fastest kids in his age group through eighth grade. When it came time to try out for freshman baseball he refused. I tried everything and believe me I mean *everything*, to get him to try out. Being the strong-willed kid he is, he got his way.

I have to confess, I was pretty bummed out that his (*and my*) baseball career came to a screeching and abrupt halt. Bottom line is Charlie told me he had a good experience playing baseball but it's *boring*. You stand around and sometimes you can go inning after inning and not be involved in any plays and when you're competing against talented pitching, you might only bat once over three innings. He said "If it weren't for you coaching, I would have given it up sooner." At first, I took that as a compliment and later realized it was *my* dream for him to play baseball and not *his* own.

Charlie decided to go out for lacrosse instead and really enjoyed it as he did varsity hockey. All's well that ends well. I'm proud of him for not just trying to please me and deciding what was right for him.

Our kids are not here to live out our unfulfilled dreams and make up for time we lost over the years by participating in every sport known to mankind. While there is great value to the lessons that sports can teach they, or any other activity, shouldn't be pushed on any kid unless they are ready, willing and genuinely interested in whatever it might be. While you might think endless hours of piano lessons are a good idea and something you enjoyed, unless your son or daughter is really onboard, it can be a liability in the long run.

Finally, if you have ever watched or attended a NASCAR race you can't help but notice the first lap has a "pace car" that is leading the pack. Those high powered machines need something to connect with speed-wise, since they don't have speedometers like regular cars. So the pace car, which is of a civilian make and model, gives them a "starting point," for the race by cruising along at 55 mph. Once all the drivers are in the order they are supposed to be, the pace car driver flips on his lights, peels off the track, the green flag drops and the race is on.

So what or who is your "pace car?" What is it you can gauge your speed and distance on while navigating the pulse pounding, straight-a-ways, the banked curves and inevitable pit stops that are part of being a dad?

Finding and maintaining a pace that works for you might not get you to the winners circle every time, but it will go a long way in assuring you finish strong and, as a dad, that is what it's all about.

Four

Don't Drink Any Water

"Who you are speaks so loudly I can't hear what you are saying."
—Ralph Waldo Emerson

The seven years after my parents divorced were somewhat traumatic. Even though I was only six years old, I remember the police being involved with domestic disputes and being dragged downtown to the courts at the Daley Center regarding custody and child-support issues. I lived with my grandparents for part of that time and went to different schools. I give my mom a lot of credit for raising me, and my younger brother Ron, on her own working as a Chicago Public School teacher. It's one of the reasons I have so much respect for single moms.

While my father wasn't present much from the time when I was six through 13, I thank God for my maternal grandfather, Sam Solomon, for being there. He was the first in his family, who immigrated to America in 1907, to be born in the U.S. Growing up during the depression shaped his character and those of his generation. I think the fact he lost his own father at 13 provided him with extra compassion for our circumstances. He was a man of principle and deeply devoted to his family. He understood the importance of education, hard work and self-sacrifice. Most of all, I remember him having a positive attitude and a gift for telling stories and jokes. While at times it felt like my life was falling apart this incredible man helped me hold it together, and so much of what I learned from him guides me today.

With access to the Internet, there is no shortage of information in the 21st century. Matter of fact there might be too much information, which can lead to a vast landfill full of conflicting advice, especially when it comes to parenting. It's part of the reason I am offering this resume of my experience as a father of five, not some "theory" based on studies but "reality" based on my experiences. When you are attempting to do something you have not done before, seeking out some respected resources is a smart thing to do. It's not every day a middle-aged, desk bound, white-collar guy hops on his bicycle for a 21-day, 2,300+ mile ride.

As I mentioned, prior to the two months of training for the Dads Honor Ride, I had completed only one century ride (100 miles in one day), five years earlier at age 48. With that in mind I fully understood the importance of learning from those more experienced, so I reached out to some neighbors who had done some endurance riding to ask for advice. That circle of friends reached out to friends of friends and beyond.

Once I mentioned I was contemplating riding Route 66 at a pace of 100+ miles a day, virtually everyone mentioned the importance of hydration. The common wisdom was drinking four to six liters of water a day to avoid being side-lined by dehydration. The point being you don't even realize you're perspiring when you are riding 12–20 mph since the wind is wicking away your sweat.

There was one lone dissenting opinion about the importance of water, offered by Lon Haldeman, one of the country's most preeminent endurance cyclists of all time. I met Lon less than two months before the Dads Honor Ride, as I was starting to ride outdoors on my new shadow grey Cannondale Synapse road bike. Lon acknowledged hydration is important, but so is nutrition. He said at the pace and distance being contemplated I could expect to burn 8,000 to 10,000 calories a day. His advice, contrary to everyone else, was "don't drink any water" but instead always consume the highest amount of calories via any liquids. Given the fact he has done more than 85 cross-country rides, including Route 66, 25 times, his words of wisdom carried a lot of weight. I'm very thankful for his advice and having followed it. I barley drank a glass of water once every couple of days, instead relying on 1,000+ calorie shakes 3x per day for both hydration and nutrition in addition to eating breakfast, lunch, dinner and snacking throughout the day.

So you might say, in this case, "common sense" (*drink a lot of water so you can stay afloat*) would not apply to my circumstances. I went to a resource that had the experience needed for me to make a decision that would allow me to reach my goal.

Being a great father is no different.

When a man becomes a dad for the first or even second, third, fourth or fifth time, as in my case, each of those children came in with their own unique blueprint that is part of me, part of their mother and part of the DNA of all the family that came before them. They are also born with a measured dose of their own self, an emerging part of the soul that, hopefully, never stops growing.

I often think of my grandfather Sam and how critical his presence was to give me an option, an image, an imprint of what a "father figure" could be as a positive role model. If I had followed in the steps of my father surely my life would be far different than it is now, and I would not likely be the man and the father I am today.

But for many men that is exactly what they do. They walk in the same footprints their father did, without questioning why or challenging the notion that our children constantly are giving us the opportunity to change and grow into bigger shoes.

Even though I had my grandfather as part of my life, the concept of "father absence" really hit home for me—*literally*—in the fall of 1996. I was 36 years old and we'd just had our fifth child in seven years. I was working full time while Peggy held down the fort, which I consider a much more challenging experience than managing investment portfolios. I was also finishing up a multi-year experience as a W.K. Kellogg Foundation national fellow, which required a commitment of three months a year for three years. I traveled periodically nationally and abroad during that time, which also included the birth of two of our children. As the fellowship was winding down I was feeling some pressure at work, but even more at home, due to the nine months I had committed to the fellowship. The massive amount of stress was a toxic byproduct of the situation. I realized I needed to redirect a good portion of time and energies to my family, being a better father to my kids and husband to Peggy.

While true, that was just the surface stuff. The real reason I was looking for fatherhood resources, was . . . *fear.*

Fear . . . that I wouldn't have a strong relationship with my kids. Fear . . . that history would repeat itself. Fear . . . that this issue of father absence would somehow undermine my relationship with my kids, as it did with me and my dad and I witnessed what it did with my dad and his dad. Fear . . . that my absence, might create a divide with my children in their formative years as my father's created in mine, a gap that might never be closed, a wound that may never heal. I realized there was this baggage of father absence being passed down from one generation to the next. I was determined not to pass this burden on down to my kids. The solution was to find resources on how to be a better father.

I benefited from the advice of more experienced riders to help me reach my goal of completing the 2,300+ miles from Santa Monica to Chicago without becoming dehydrated. On my quest to avoid passing the baggage of father absence to my kids, I began to dig through mountains of material on fatherhood, and my search brought me to an incredible individual who not only gave me a guidepost towards my goal, but also opened my eyes to the extraordinary challenge faced by a society where tens of millions of children go through life without a father.

Enter Dr. Ken Canfield, author of several books including *Heart Of A Father, They Call Me Dad* and *The Seven Secrets of Effective Fathers.* He is also the founder of the National Center for Fathering (NCF), a Kansas City-based nonprofit, and was also the father of five kids, so the connection went even deeper.

Through Dr. Canfield and his work at NCF, I learned some shocking statistics—four out of 10 kids, approximately 24 million children (half boys and half girls)—are growing up in "father-absent homes" and an estimated 500,000 are born every year with the line on their birth certificate where "Father" should be named . . . blank.

In October of 2015, I was privileged to make a TEDx presentation—the locally produced version of the world-wide TED (Technology, Entertainment and Design) program. My talk was entitled "Why We Need to Break The Cycle of Father Absence." In the time it takes to deliver a TED Talk (18 minutes), 145 children are born in the United States. If nothing changes, 58 of them will grow up in father-absent homes. That translates into three per minute, 193 per hour and a jaw-dropping 4,640 youth born EVERY DAY, who will grow up without their dad.

Number of U.S. Kids Who Will Live Without Dads

Born every minute 3
Born every hour 193
Born every day 4,640

Sadly, children from father-absent homes are four times more likely to grow up in poverty and nine times more likely to drop out of high school. This is nothing short of an epidemic with dire consequences for too many of these kids, their families and society at-large.

Furthermore, 3,200+ youth drop out of high school EVERY DAY across the United States. Pathetically, the U.S. ranks #22 out of the top 27 developed countries for the percentage of youth who graduate from high school.

Consider that 71% of the youth who drop out of high school are from father-absent homes. A whopping 75% of all the crimes committed in the United States are by high school dropouts while 85% of incarcerated youth come from *father-absent* homes.

These dots are not hard to connect.

Our culture has been shifting away from marriage and families for decades. Consider that in 1971 pre-marital births (the more modern term for "out of wedlock births") were 11% of the population, compared with 41% today. Don't shoot the messenger, but you're not getting that genie back in the bottle. The return to a more "traditional" family structure in America is unlikely. While numbers often fluctuate, the fact is, in just a few decades, the concept of fathers becoming an extinct species is setting too many kids on a collision course, almost subconsciously, with a greater possibility of a lifetime of violence, crime, broken dreams and unanswered prayers.

My response to learning about the scope and scale of the problem, prompted me to organize a community leaders briefing at the Union League Club of Chicago in February, 1997. I invited Dr. Canfield, Mike Singletary (the former Super Bowl XX Chicago Bears player and now Hall of Fame member) along with a handful of national and local experts, to speak. We were pleased 120 community leaders attended and affirmed the message for more involved fathering and Illinois Fatherhood Initiative (IFI), the country's first state-wide, nonprofit fatherhood organization was born. IFI's mission is connecting children and fathers. Over the past 19 years, more than 400,000 youth have written essays about their dads, stepdads, grand-dads, and father-figures as part of the annual fatherhood essay contest.

Annually, IFI engages upwards of 800 volunteers; men and women, aged 18–90 from very diverse ethnic and socio-economic backgrounds, to come together to evaluate what today's youth have to say about their dads, stepdads, granddad and father-figures. The essay reading has proven to be such a profound experience that some of the essays are reprinted in the *Me & My Dad* essay booklet (see information in Resources to obtain a copy). Very early on (actually the first year) seven of the students who wrote essays were selected by the folks at Harpo Productions to read their essays for a special program about fathers on *The Oprah Winfrey Show*. I actually appeared on the *Oprah* show along with my then 88-year-old maternal grandfather. It was a surreal experience, and one of our most memorable grandfather/grandson moments.

One of the takeaways from the essay contest is the most direct way to reach the heart of a father is through the words of his children.

If the ripple effect of father absence had negative consequences, we knew creating the same effect with a different result was possible, to offset the negative with a positive.

With the benefit of hindsight, creating IFI was not only cathartic in healing my own absent father wounds, but in many ways it became a great way to honor the presence of my maternal grandfather. Grandpa Sam, who mostly by his example, helped shape my character and taught me some fundamental lessons about fathering including: commitment, honesty, love and patience.

Remember you don't always have to drink water to stay hydrated and there are a myriad of ways to stay healthy on the journey, be it across a desert or across the dinner table. Getting great advice is one thing, putting it into action is another.

At my grandfather's funeral in April of 2001, I read this quote by Ralph Waldo Emerson: "Who you are speaks so loudly, I can't hear what you are saying." While my Grandpa Sam certainly gave me plenty of advice over the years, it was who he was, and the example he set, that had the greatest impact on me. Thanks, Gramps!

Five

With Your Wings & My Legs

Blessed indeed is the man who hears many gentle voices call him father!
—Lydia M. Child

Let's be candid, I'm athletic, but I'm not an athlete. I was a one-sport athlete in high school playing varsity baseball. Truth be told, I was the backup catcher and caught more splinters than games in my senior year. I played intramural sports in college. Since then I've done a handful of marathons and half marathons as well as a dozen and a half, mostly Olympic distance triathlons, always finishing in the lower end of my age-group.

So it makes no sense at all at 54, an age where most men are starting to slow down a bit, I am beginning to speed up. Riding my bicycle across half the United States, I am shifting gears, powering uphill and maneuvering the curves, which I have encountered not only on the road, but also as a father.

The road is rarely straight, or the lines clearly painted and there are not many signposts pointing the way to being a 21st century dad. I have made more than my share of mistakes over the years raising my children. When I have fallen short of what I could be, I remember that perfection does not exist, but improvement is always an option. I don't have all the answers but, just like those very tough and long days pedaling my way in the rain, the wind and or blazing sun, when I came to the end of my resources I would put my faith in God and repeat to myself, multiple times a day, "With Your wings and my legs we're going the distance."

Faith has many definitions but for me, what St. Augustine declared somewhere around 400 AD rings true: "Faith is to believe in what you do not see; the reward of this faith is to see what you have believed."

On one hand, given my background and career, it defied logic to don a helmet and skin-tight riding gear, line up a route that took me 2,300+ miles in just 21 days, through eight states from California to Illinois. I wasn't alone on this journey. Most days, I was accompanied by other riders who also helped raise money and awareness for fatherhood charities. I also had my faith to keep me company.

As a father, faith is essential when it comes to making a positive impact.

Even though you map the route out, you can anticipate there will be flat tires, blisters, exhaustion and a bit of pain along the way. Not unlike being a dad, you do your best to plan the journey, the guide book if you will, when it comes to being present; spiritually, financially, emotionally and physically (The Quadrant—*remember?*).

Those four elements, at least for me, have all been connected by faith, which has slowly been evolving over the years, making me a better husband, father and human being.

So it is faith I call on when I cannot see the road ahead. I am suggesting to you an essential ingredient for being a fully engaged father is a sense of something greater than yourself, something you can lean on and learn from, something to guide you when your past limits your future. It's like a "GPS" allowing you to envision the road ahead, to stay on the right course and avoid making mistakes. In the natural world, this is beyond our understanding and physical boundaries. It's called *Putting on the Whole Armor of God*.

It was June 4th, our fourth day on the road and, arguably, one of the toughest days of the Dads Honor Ride. After persevering 394 miles the first three days in 100-degree temperatures in the California and Arizona deserts, I had to tackle the 6,500-foot climb up to Prescott, Arizona. One of the challenges for completing the ride was putting in suitable training for the steep climbs, since there is nowhere in the Chicago area to adequately prepare for climbing those distances. As we reached downtown Prescott there was nowhere to park our 28-foot RV. Addie, my 18-year-old daughter (and youngest of our five kids), was piloting the RV along with her 89-year-old co-pilot and fellow crew member Lawton "Wilk" Wilkerson, our friend and WWII veteran from the south suburbs of Chicago. We decided to temporarily pull over in a no parking zone to get our bearings before heading out of town for the remaining 43 miles to Cottonwood, Arizona, our destination.

We weren't there for more than five minutes when this surfer dude, with bulging muscles, tattoos, a barrel chest, a tight fitting t-shirt, comfy jeans and flip flops walks up to inquire what we're doing. Long story short, Tim Parker identifies himself as the executive director of the Set Free Center, one of the country's premiere drug and alcohol centers, serving four thousand youth a year. He also mentioned he's a former U.S. Marine and the father of four, so naturally, I got out a Great Dads Coin, (you can find out more about the coins in the back of the book) and make a heartfelt presentation passing along the Great Dads Coin in a handshake. He was so moved by the experience, he pulled a *Whole Armor of God* coin from his pocket and proceeded to make his own heart-felt presentation from Ephesians, including a detailed description about each aspect of the armor, including  the helmet, sword, breast-plate, loin cover, boots and shield. That lead to me introducing him to Wilk, the former WWII aviator and Tuskegee Airman. Before I knew it, Tim pulled a USMC coin from another pocket and presented it to Wilk in a touching tear-filled presentation.

A random encounter in downtown Prescott, Arizona, with Tim Parker, executive director of the Set Free Center, who presented me with the Whole Armor of God coin.

Before departing, Tim insisted on praying for our safe passage the next 17 days. So, there the four of us stood, in the middle of downtown Prescott, arms on one another's shoulders as Tim offered his heartfelt prayers. I've carried that *Whole Armor of God* coin with me every day since June 4, 2015, as a reminder of the encounter and to carry the *Whole Armor of God* every day of my life.

As one father to another, I want to share with you (and to Mothers reading this, as well) the absolute certainty I have come to understand that having the guiding principle of God in my life has been the catalyst for miracles. It is what allows me to keep pushing forward, no matter how big the obstacle might be, either on the road or with one of my children. As my faith has grown so has my ability to become a better father, distancing myself from the chains of the past and ensuring none of my children will have to spend time wondering, as I did, whether or not my father cared.

As a father, consider adopting the mindset that originated with the Native America Iroquois, which is known as the "Great Law of the Iroquois" or "Seven Generation Sustainability," which holds us accountable and says to think seven generations ahead (which is about 140 years) and decide whether the decisions we make today would benefit our family seven generations into the future.

Oren Lyons, Chief of the Onondaga Nation, writes: "We are looking ahead, as is one of the first mandates given us as chiefs, to make sure and to make every decision that we make relate to the welfare and well-being of the seventh generation to come. . . ."

"What about the seventh generation? Where are you taking them? What will they have?"

That is the power you have as a father or perhaps "the Chief" and figurehead of your family. That is what you are being called to do, rise above that which holds you back and move forward with faith as your rudder, instead of fear.

In John 14:10 Jesus declares "Believest thou not that I am in the Father, and the Father in me? The words that I speak unto you I speak not of myself: but the Father that dwelleth in me, he doeth the works."

I am not alone on this honor ride and neither are you when it comes to being a great father.

The same Spirit of God that urged me forward on a 2,300+ mile journey is the same Spirit in you. It is there as a resource, a respite and a path of Resurrection when it comes to replacing your past, whatever it might be, with a brighter future that will create a ripple effect for all the generations that follow you.

It is near impossible to "be there" spiritually for your kids, if you haven't defined it for yourself, no more than being able to give them money if your account is empty. Find what fills you up from a faith standpoint, cultivate it by standing on it and let your children see it in action which, as we know, is always more important than words alone.

"With Your wings and my legs" is my prayer when heading into the wind on a long stretch of lonely highway, but it's the same thought whether or not you ever sit on a bike seat.

The road of fatherhood looks different for each of us, but faith is the one constant force that will allow you to overcome, endure and cross the finish line a better man than when you started the journey, the day your child was born.

Six
The Strength & Influence of Spokes

My father didn't tell me how to live; he lived and let me watch him do it.
—Clarence Budington Kelland

The handlebars on the bike underneath me have become an extension of my anatomy, as has the frame I ride become part of my skeletal system. The fusion of man and machine is almost like a work of art, one working off the other, both capable of greater distance, one needing the other to succeed in this journey.

With so many miles ahead of me, and a substantial amount behind me, my mind finds interesting and creative ways to keep busy. While my legs keep pumping on the pedals, I think of my kids, Peggy, work, baseball, anything and everything to push past the barriers that crop up in an effort like this, where my body is fully engaged and the space between my ears often wanders. Mile after mile there seems to be no end to the amount of information passing through my mind. Not far from my thoughts are the dads, as I pass near or through a town, I see them with their children. There are glimpses of grandfathers, those men who carried the load for their children and now watch their grandchildren through somewhat different eyes. Then there are those who, in so many ways, have taken on the mission to become a "father figure" filling in where another dad was unable or unwilling to ensure the next generation has the resources and spirit to offset the erosion that previous generations might have caused, a closing of the gap between a man and a child.

That sort of commitment is a calling of the highest order, and it's a calling to serve at a level few will ever respond to, but I know one man who did.

Peter Spokes.

With a BA from Yale and MBA from Stanford, Peter spent more than fourteen years at General Mills, Inc. where he served as Vice President in consumer product marketing and eventually president of Yoplait. His ability to create and lead made him a valuable asset in the for-profit world, but something was missing in his life.

He found that *something* in the work of the National Center for Fathering (NCF), the nonprofit organization created by Dr. Ken Canfield who I mentioned previously. So in 1994, Peter and his wife, Barbara, packed up their six kids (ages 8–14) and moved their family from his hometown of Minneapolis to Kansas City as executive vice-president of NCF.

With his business acumen and professionalism, he was able help guide and direct NCF's effort, bringing forth his considerable marketing skills to reach the "dad demographic" eventually becoming Chief Operating Officer. Among his many contributions, Peter greatly influenced the development of NCF's website, fathers.com, and he was a key player in creating the nation's first "Fathering Court Program" for non-custodial fathers in Kansas City.

Peter became a respected fathering advocate on the national stage. He served on the National Conference of State Legislator's Advisory Committee on Responsible Fatherhood, the National Fatherhood Leaders Group and on President Obama's Advisory Council on Faith-Based Initiatives and Neighborhood Partnerships Task Force on Fatherhood and Healthy Families. Besides his passion for helping dads, he also had a heart for the fatherless and was a father figure to many beyond his own six children.

We first met in the fall of 1996 at a meeting of fatherhood advocates held in Minneapolis and convened by the Ford Foundation. Dr. Canfield and Peter were two of a dozen plus experts in attendance. I was merely a dad looking for fatherhood resources with the objective of becoming a better dad. Peter and I hit it off from the very beginning. We spoke the same language as businessmen and shared some of the same experiences being fathers of six and five children respectively.

Ken and Peter were the two who inspired me to create the Illinois Fatherhood Initiative in 1997, the country's first state-wide nonprofit fatherhood organization. My relationship with Peter would span the first 14 years of IFI, during which time we forged a strong partnership between NCF and IFI. Along the way we also developed a meaningful friendship. Every one of our conversations always started with a run down of what was going on with our families, the fun highlights and some candid reflections on the challenges we were encountering. Since there was an eight year difference in age between us and the ages of our kids, I was the primary benefactor of those conversations, listening and learning about some of the challenges that lay ahead.

One of my favorite memories, what I affectionately refer to as "Spokisms," was the insight Peter shared with me about keeping a couple of Band-Aids in my wallet. He said one way to have your young children reach out to you when they are hurt is to carry a couple of Band-Aids. When they skin their knee or cut themselves, which is inevitable, they will naturally seek you out if they know you have a Band-Aid. This reaching out when they were young morphed as they became older into their reaching out to me when the issues became more consequential than a bruised elbow or knee. Do as I do—to this day—and keep a Band-Aid in your wallet. It could have a more profound impact than you might imagine.

Peter was a quiet force and what drove him was a great depth of faith, that he was put on this earth to do more than sit behind a desk at a major corporation. He had a vision that if 10 percent of the 65 million dads (at that time) in the U.S. began living the commitment of becoming a "Championship Father" the ripple effect of these 6.5 million men would go well beyond their immediate families and impact generations to come. Peter calculated those men, standing shoulder to shoulder would span the distance between Boston and San Diego.

As we kicked off Dads Honor Ride in Santa Monica, I had a pretty fair idea of how impressive a line of men would look like, standing shoulder to shoulder, and stretching from coast to coast. It's that sort of vision Peter brought to the forefront of fathering, a critical mass of men influencing their sons and daughters in a way generations before them had not.

Perhaps that is why Peter's leukemia diagnosis in 2009 was all the more difficult to accept.

After several attempts to battle the disease, including a bone marrow transplant, radiation and chemo therapy, Peter came to the conclusion, based on his deep faith, this was God's will for his life. He decided to suspend the heroic effort the doctors were making to save his life, so he could live out whatever time he had left immersed in the joy of his family.

Peter J. Spokes passed away on May 24, 2010. He was 57 years old.

When I heard the news of his death, something inside me cracked open, I felt an overwhelming urge to attend his funeral service and celebration of life in Kansas City. The width and depth of his life, his unending commitment to fatherhood and the impact he made was on full display. Tribute after tribute painted a picture of a man who had answered the call. The long-time family priest from Minneapolis gave a very personal eulogy as did the pastor from their church in Kansas City.

I sat in the rear of the packed service with tears streaming down my face but it wasn't until two of his children spoke that the *essence* of Peter became clear to me. But first, let me share a small insight about his name that helped me think of Peter in another way.

When bicycle wheels are built, the *spokes* must have the precise length or the threads might be engaged in the rim, which would actually create a weaker wheel if too short, or stick through the rim and possibly puncture the inner tube causing a flat tire.

During Dads Honor Ride 2015 I had ten flats, in about as many days, before switching to a set of Continental Ultra GatorSkin tires. So while the *spokes* don't look very important they are critical to maintaining the integrity and strength of the rim. They support my weight on the wheel itself and, even more important, *they transfer the power* of my legs from the crankshaft to the back wheel, making these seemingly metal spaghetti like rods a critical piece of moving forward.

Perhaps most important of all, the *spokes don't push outward* as it might seem at first glance, but rather the *spokes pull the rim inward* towards the hub, making it extremely strong where it counts . . . at the center. Finally, because of the way *spokes* are designed, it's all about weight distribution. Even under heavy loads, the weight is distributed evenly, and doesn't put too much *pressure on any one spoke.*

That's what Peter Spokes did. He pulled so many men, looking for their center, inward towards his vision, towards the hub of fatherhood. Through his unending faith in God, he demonstrated the process of becoming a better father and his unwavering commitment to key principles that any man can put to use that ensure a better future for his family. Peter took on a great load of responsibility, not just as COO at The National Center for Fathering, but devoted husband to Barbara and super dad of six children; Pete, Erin, Megan, Annie, Charlie and Tim.

His essence . . . was the reminder that *as fathers we are not alone.* That we do not have to bear the load by ourselves, that there are many "spokes" in the world that can help us not break under pressure, or throw our wheel out of balance. Again, I urge you to seek out and "draft behind" fathers with older kids and to use the resources listed at the end of this book. Reaching out and up is the first step towards finding the ingredients needed to be a 21st century dad.

As I sat in the back of the church at Peter's funeral service, moved by all the words and memories, it was the voices of two of his children, Pete and Megan, who had the most profound impact. While they were sad their father had passed away, they were very much at peace. It was a remarkable situation. Here they were, their father's body lying nearby in his casket, speaking on behalf of their siblings, giving the most powerful testimony children could offer a father. Their love and gratitude were palpable as they described their dad's ongoing involvement in their lives; attending all the sporting events, recitals, plays and family dinners. He took his family on memorable vacations and made sure to celebrate each of their 21st birthdays with a beer, glass of wine or drink.

But the real source of their strength and serenity was their spirituality. In addition to *being* there for them in this world, he was their spiritual leader teaching them by his word and deed what it meant to be a Christian by adhering to his principles as a loving husband, devoted father, good friend to so many and a man of obedient faith to his Heavenly Father.

While I knew Peter to be a man of faith, I was not prepared for the depth of the impact his spirituality had on his children. There was that "popping" sound again. A switch flipped and a light bulb was set aglow, becoming brighter and brighter, shining a light on my own spirituality, or more accurately my lack of spirituality.

By all outward observations the Hirschs were a model Christian family. We baptized and christened each of our five children. They each attended Catholic school, first through eighth grade. They each became altar servers and eventually ecumenical ministers. We attended Church on a weekly basis with rare exception. Peggy was president of the women's board at the church and super involved at St. Anne School for well over a dozen years. I initiated the Watch D.O.G.S. (Dads Of Great Students) inspiring dozens and dozens of dads per semester to take a day off from work to volunteer in their child's school and doing the same myself for a 10 year period of time. I even took a week off work to serve as a chaperone on a teen mission trip to Kentucky.

This is a long-winded way of emphasizing by all outward observation the Hirschs were a model Christian family, with one small exception.

I was not a Christian.

For anyone paying close attention this was no big secret. While we attended weekly Mass, mom and dad sitting side-by-side, with the idea our kids would never be able to say, "Why do I have to go if Dad doesn't go to Church?"

The *only* thing Dad didn't do was go up to receive Communion.

Sitting there in the pew at Peter's funeral, I was overwhelmed with the thought I didn't share a spiritual relationship with my children. I wasn't the spiritual leader to my children that Peter had been to his. What would the impact on them be? How could I have been spiritually asleep all these years and not realized it? What could I do about it? My mind was spinning.

Fortunately, Peggy had done a fabulous job as our family's spiritual leader.

Everyone at the reception after Peter's funeral service was remarking what a beautiful service it was, especially the eulogies by Pete and Megan. I remember talking with those present and thinking the whole plane ride home that I needed to do something about the spiritual void in my life. After recounting the experience for Peggy, she simply said "Maybe you should talk to a priest."

As I thought about it, the fear of the unknown started to creep in. Would I put myself "in play" if I talked to a priest in our own parish? I chose a less threatening route. I decided to reach out to Father Britto Berchmans, senior pastor at St. Paul of the Cross Church in Mt. Prospect, 20 miles away. Britto had been our associate pastor years earlier, a family friend and is a very approachable guy.

Over lunch a week later, Britto's most memorable remark was, "It's taken you the first 49 years of your life to get to this point, let's not do something hastily in the wake of your friend's death." He gave me a pile of books to read and suggested I visit the public library and checkout additional titles that peaked my curiosity with instructions to reconvene in two months.

The next two months whizzed by. At our follow-up breakfast it was readily apparent the spiritual signal had not faded, but had actually grown stronger. As Britto described the RCIA (The Rite of Christian Initiation of Adults) process, I expressed my reluctance to draw attention to myself with anything to do with religion. After all, my Jewish grandfather who passed nine years earlier, had always instructed me not to be outspoken about religion and politics.

Britto explained he would not be able to be my RCIA sponsor. That was not the way it worked in the Catholic Church. I would have to find a layperson to serve as my sponsor. He redirected me to meet with Sister Anna Marie Dressier in my own parish.

There I was a few days later, sitting in the living room of this super friendly 70+ year old nun's home learning about the RCIA program. After a brief meeting, and an invitation to attend the upcoming weekly Monday evening meeting, I was on my way. Upon arriving home Peggy was curious how the meeting went and a bit surprised to learn I had signed her up to be my sponsor.

The next eight months flew by. There were 12 of us, two catechumens (including myself) and 10 candidates in the group, each of us on his or her own spiritual journey linked together by our weekly RCIA meetings. At the Easter Vigil on April 23, 2011, I was baptized and confirmed with all the sins from the first 50 years of my life absolved. I was born a Jew and now was a neophyte Christian.

When you answer the call, you are not just changing your life, but all those who will come after you. Six years after Peter passed away, I still tear up thinking about the impact his faith had on his family, myself and countless others, as well as the enormous impact of his advocacy for fathers.

As it says in Timothy 4:7 "I have fought a good fight, I have finished my course, I have kept the faith."

Peter's impact continues well after his death. The question is . . . how will you be remembered as a father?

Seven

No Matter What

"America used to live by the motto 'Father Knows Best.' Now we're lucky if 'Father Knows He Has Children.' We've become a nation of sperm donors and baby daddies."
—Stephen Colbert

When I was growing up, the dads on television looked like Robert Young (*Father Knows Best*) Ralph Waite (John Walton, Sr. on *The Waltons*) Danny Thomas (*Make Room for Daddy*) and, of course, Andy Griffith who doled out fatherly advice to Opie back in Mayberry. In that lineup you could include a slew of other "dads" that all brought something different, yet somehow familiar to their roles. Michael Landon kept things in order on *Little House on the Prairie*, Howard Cunningham (Tom Bosley) handled duties as the "go to guy" on *Happy Days* and Redd Foxx brought a comedic genius to the role of Fred G. Sanford on *Sanford and Son* as did Carroll O'Connor, the knuckle dragging, bigoted and heavy-handed Archie Bunker on *All in the Family*.

Unfortunately, with the advent of "reality television," today's kids often see a very different portrayal of the role of fathers and the family in general. Sadly, the audience for shows that exploit broken homes, abhorrent behavior and damaged relationships has grown, fueled by a side show mentality that does nothing to offset the real challenges of being a father.

Much of this started with *The Jerry Springer Show* that boasts a warning before each episode "May Contain Content Not Appropriate For Children," which as we all know only becomes of more interest to kids and does little or nothing to stop young minds from watching and inhaling bad behavior. For over two decades, a steady stream of the lowest human activity possible has been on display and ready for download to its audience. But it was Maury Povich who really capitalized on the very things I am riding to bring awareness to: Father absence, broken homes, disconnected kids. Those themes, however, mean something very different in the world of "entertainment."

Beginning in 2008, the *Maury* show has fed audiences a diet of paternity and lie detector tests that results in a steady stream of young men and women who battle back and forth until the moment of climax when Maury opens up a manila envelope and announces one of two conclusions.

"You *are not* the father!" or "You *are* the father!"

Both of these proclamations bring about a reaction not just from the audience, but the young mother. Endless episodes reveal that "You *are not* the father!" and a young woman breaks down on the stage while the audience shout obscene words, until she runs backstage in tears, all the while followed by a television camera, of course. The young men break out into a celebratory dance as music blares in the studio. Suddenly *off the hook*, they have had their 15 minutes of fame for all the wrong reasons. Conversely, "You *are* the father!" creates more mayhem as the young man realizes in front of a national audience he is now *on the hook* and responsible for the life of a child, and most of these "now proclaimed fathers" are barely past adolescences themselves.

More mayhem, of course, ensues.

Stuck in the middle of all this terrible energy surrounding people, who are in need of some great mentors and serious counseling, is a child, a little boy or girl, who without their consent have their faces splayed on a giant screen in the studio, while both sides bicker over what the future looks like, which is most likely bleak, at best, for all of them.

So while it's true, on some level, the drama is jacked up for television, the *Maury* Show sheds light on some very dark corners that will continue to become even darker as this type of activity gets fed and rewarded over and over again, as it has since some producer got the bright idea there is an audience for dysfunctional family dynamics.

The show is a constant reminder to me that Dads Honor Ride, and all that goes along with it, is needed now more than ever. Something a country boy turned writer, turned producer was also convinced of.

On March 24, 2016, Earl Hamner, Jr. passed away at the age of 92. He was the creator and executive producer of *The Waltons* that aired on TV for nine seasons and garnered more than a dozen Emmys for the show that mirrored his family and formative years growing up in Schuyler, Virginia, during the Great Depression. In sharp contrast to all the negative ways family is splayed out on television in the 21st century, *The Waltons* focused on the many ways a family can overcome adversity, loss, death and yet celebrate in simple yet profound ways.

As Hamner wrote in the *LA Times*: "Audiences in all entertainment media have been brutalized by crudities, vulgarity, violence, indifference and ineptitude. With *The Waltons*, we are attempting to make an honest, positive statement on the affirmation of man."

That was in 1972, 44 years ago. While the television landscape has changed, the foundational aspects of family have not.

A television show that attempted to affirm our higher nature. What a concept! The good news is you can still find John-Boy and the rest of the Waltons on various channels living in eternal syndication.

So borrowing a line from Povich let me say this clearly as I can "You *are* the father . . . No matter what!"

If you are in a situation as a single dad, from divorce especially, your primary function is really very simple.

Be there . . . *no matter what.* Keep your word . . . *no matter what . . .* Listen to your children . . . *no matter what . . .* set the highest example you possibly can by your actions and not just your words . . . *no matter what.*

The circumstances that find us becoming fathers range from the traditional "Let's have a baby" to "Uh . . . guess what?" to "SURPRISE!" and everything in-between. How you became a father isn't nearly as important as accepting the full responsibility that you are one. If you haven't figured it out by now, children don't always hear what you say but digest everything you do. Actions always speak louder than words and if we are to break the chains that create a lineup of guests on ranting talk shows, then we have to get ourselves in order . . . *no matter what.*

As Henry Ford first said, and many after him: "If you always do what you've always done, you will always get what you've always got." When applied to being a father, your test subjects are your children and the test "results" will show up in the way they conduct their lives.

I thought it might be useful to share how Merriam-Webster's Dictionary defines "Father."

A man who has begotten a child; also:
Sire, God: the first person of the Trinity.

No pressure having the same title as the Creator of the Universe, but in so many ways the universe we create for our children puts us in a very powerful position, perhaps on a pedestal where the chances of falling off are many.

So you thought the dad thing was going to be a cakewalk eh?

Far from it, rather it's a 24/7/365 commitment that changes form and morphs over the years, but never goes away. You have to be prepared for anything and everything, not just when it's easy or the sun is shining but also for when it's hard and the storms roll in—something I learned sitting on the seat of my bike.

If you're going to be outdoors for 12 hours a day and traveling over 2,300 miles for three weeks, you have to be prepared for all types of terrain and weather, including rain. Most who are casual about exercise, are fair weather exercisers. If it's cold and or wet, we just workout indoors and avoid the elements. It dawned on me while riding six days a week for the two months leading up to the ride, I needed to get accustomed to riding in cold as well as rainy conditions. If you only workout in comfortable dry conditions, you'll be ill prepared for the real deal. To be better prepared, I bought a high end rain suit including a jacket, trousers with suspenders, a hood and rain boots.

Being prepared for rainy days is really no different than understanding that being a dad is a 24/7 type commitment. If you're serious about doing anything every day, you need to do what it takes be prepared for those cloudy, wet inclement and less than ideal situations.

In many ways doing a cross-country bike ride is a metaphor for life and also fatherhood. There are those days where you have the sun shining down on you, with the wind at your back and life is good. The sun is also like a double-edged sword. In moderation it provides us with warmth and energy. As with anything else in life, too much of a good thing can be more of a liability than an asset as witnessed by the days we rode through the desert heading east through California and into Western Arizona where the daytime temperatures in the shade were 100 degrees. Instead of providing energy, the excessive heat is actually sucking your energy away.

In the California desert, where temperatures average 106 degrees in June.

Being a father can suck your energy too, unless you are prepared to stay hydrated and fill yourself up from the inside out with the needed resources, support, guidance and commitment it takes to set an example of what's possible, no matter what the weather conditions might be.

There's an old adage that says, "if you can't stand the heat, get out of the kitchen." Sadly, when the going gets tough—i.e. the heat gets to be too much—too many dads not only leave the kitchen, they leave the house and don't return.

Committed dads need to anticipate these tough times and create a plan for persevering these oppressive occasions. If the challenges of fathering seem to be too much to handle, it's time to seek advice from more experienced riders, before reaching a breaking point. If you've already left and you're a non-custodial dad, you need to chart a different path, a new route, to ensure you're present physically and emotionally in your child's life.

Because at the end of the day or the middle of the day or the beginning of the day . . . "You *are* the father" . . . *No matter what!*

At the world-famous Gateway Arch in St. Louis; it rained almost all day.

Eight
Patience, Persistence & Purpose

If it is important to you, you will find a way, if not you will find an excuse.
—Unknown

There are dozens of obstacles to consider when preparing for a cross-country bike ride. I've already covered some of the biggies, like hydration, nutrition and seeking out expert opinions so you can emulate those who are getting it right and live vicariously through the mistakes of others, so to avoid making the same mistakes yourself.

Let's be real. It's impossible to be prepared for absolutely every occasion you'll encounter in life or on a cross-country ride. One thing you know for certain is you're going to get flat tires. It's as predictable as your teenager who starts to push back on your fatherly advice. To add a little salt to the wound, be prepared for his mother to point out "He's *your* son . . ."

When traveling long distances on a bike, or in life, you are going to encounter plenty of obstacles. So you plan and prepare as much as you can for the seen and unseen on the road ahead. When riding, debris, road kill and potholes are the obvious obstacles for getting a flat let alone being launched off your bike. The objective is to get as few flats as possible and to minimize the time to get back on the road when flats occur.

For the ride, we had a multiple point plan in place to make sure flat tires and other problems wouldn't slow us down.

Plan A—Utilizing new equipment that would be less susceptible to wearing out.

Plan B—Having an excess supply of replacement tubes, extra tires and all sorts of parts that could be swapped out on a moment's notice. Special thanks to Bob Olsen and our friends at Wheel Werks, a bike store close to home, who gave us thousands of dollars of parts, on consignment. What we used we paid for and the rest was returned. There would be no waiting and wondering if there was a local bike shop when we most needed it.

Plan C—Carry extra wheel sets, so there was no need to change tires by the side of the road. We could just pluck off the flat tire and wheel and snap in the good one and were ready to roll.

Plan D—Carry seven extra bikes in the trailer so in the event of a more serious situation, not just a flat, there was no need to stop. The extra bikes, of varying sizes, also made it convenient for those who wanted to join us along the way and avoid the inconvenience of shipping or transporting their own bike.

In total, I had 10 flats, including a double in the rain approaching Winslow. There was little or no drama when Murphy's Law paid us a visit. Being a good Scout, I just swapped the double flat bike for another and kept on pedaling.

Waiting for roadside assistance with two flats west of Winslow.

The road of life has a variety of twists and turns. Add to that the enormous responsibility of being a parent, a father, especially for the first time and every single day can be adventure or offer up some unexpected challenges. Having a road map and a destination is fine, but often times the events that take place are not on that map and even though you might have some serious back up (extra tires) you are still going to encounter challenges.

Surprisingly, I never got a flat because I hit a pothole or ran over some visible debris. Every one of the 10 flats I experienced was from those itsy bitsy pieces of metal wire that come from the inside of radial tires. You can't see them from a distance, but they are everywhere, especially when riding the interstate and other heavily trafficked roads.

Another flat, another selfie.

Over the course of the Dads Honor Ride I came up short of the day's planned destination on a couple of occasions, once due to lightning and the other due to fatigue.

I've lost count of the times I came up short as a father, especially in the early years when I was overwhelmed working full-time and going to graduate school at night. I would often lose sight of the very thin line between *reacting* and *responding*. As a dad, your buttons are going to get pushed. You also will get exhausted and overwhelmed at times, especially when the pressure is on, which is just about every day even when your kids are older. Reaction is driven by emotion; response is managed by thought. It's been said that the difference between reacting and responding is about 10 seconds, or the time it takes to let the emotion of the situation pass, and bring forth reasonable thought; a powerful tool for fathers. Let's call them the three Ps when it comes to being a father: *Patience, Persistence* and *Purpose.*

Interestingly enough, those are the very same concepts I had as a foundation when riding across half the United States. *Patience,* in accepting I could only ride so far and so fast each day. *Persistence* in getting up and on my bike every day and seeing the journey through to the next point on the map and eventually those last 37 miles from Monee, Illinois, to U.S. Cellular Field, home of the Chicago White Sox. *Purpose,* never losing sight of my vision, my goal and commitment . . . for that is what allowed me to be patient and persistent. They are all connected.

But back to how important those three "P's" are as a dad.

Patience, as it has been said, is a virtue, and no more is that true then when it comes to being a father. When your children are small, it's easy to forget (like I did at times) that they are "humans in the making" and many experts insist the first decade of a child's life determines to a great degree how they will "see" the rest of their lives. A healthy self-esteem is essential to living a full and rich life. With so many negative influences and messages, which are counterproductive to a strong sense of self-worth, the last thing your kids need from you as their father is to be overly critical and over bearing when it comes to your communication and connection with them.

As I have pointed out before, this might be the biggest hurdle you face personally, if you grew up with parents that were less than supportive and had no real sense of their own self-worth.

Every day as a 21st century dad, you have the opportunity to make sure the debilitating and destructive habits that might have been part of your formative years are not injected into your children.

So patience with your sons and daughters is *critical* . . . and so is patience *with yourself.* That's right. You have to be patient with yourself because the stressors, obligations and commitments you shoulder are formidable. To understand that you don't have to "do it all" or even "be it all." You just have to commit to making the changes necessary and taking the steps needed to live up to your fullest and true potential as a father.

Secondly, you have to develop a *persistence* to offset your kid's *resistance.*

Believe it or not, at some point your kids are going to think you are the least evolved human who ever walked the earth, some sort of cosmic blob that by random luck ended up making your way in the world and all of your ideas, advice and insight doesn't amount to a bucket of dead bugs. There will come a time when your kids know it all . . . or *think* they do.

This is when they actually need you the most, but pretend they don't even care you exist.

Don't take it personally, just gently persist as need be. Imagine the concept of "bumper bowling" where the gutters on a bowling lane are filled with a long padded tube. When the ball goes toward the gutter, it comes right back out, gently guided down the lanes to the pins.

It isn't about not letting your kids throw gutter balls, because there are valuable lessons in losing, but it's about being willing to stand in the gutter a bit and make sure they stay on course.

That takes persistence to withstand their resistance. Let your unconditional love be the rudder that steers the ship. Don't let the emotions at the surface fill your sails with anger, which can create words between you and your children that, once spoken, can create chasms that might take a very long time to close.

The third P is all about Purpose.

Not your purpose career-wise but rather your intent, your aim or goal, the very reason why you are called "father" by your children.

Are you mindful about the values and concepts you are teaching your children either consciously or even more importantly unconsciously? Kids have incredible radar AND sonar, watching and listening to everything, especially their parents. So, if you struggle with something and they are witness to it, you can rest assured how you handle whatever the challenge might be is pretty much setting up the blueprint for the exact same response from your kids when it's their time to be tested. How you and your wife (or children's mother) communicate, relate and interact with each other is basically a crash course in human relationships they will carry into their adult lives, unless something comes along to alter their behavior.

I am going to get off the psychological stump here, because this book isn't really about doing some "on the couch" therapy session but rather to simply underscore the concept that "lessons are repeated until learned . . . and the learning never ends." That truth applies to crossing the country on a bike, building a career or relationship and certainly to the role of a "21st Century Dad."

Nine

The Great Divide

The most important thing a father can do for his children is to love their mother.
—Theodore Hesburg

The sights, the sounds and the incredible energy of pushing my bike across miles of highways and byways were a constant and welcome companion on my trek.

With my support vehicle not far behind, I didn't need to concern myself with regard to any emergency or a break that might be needed. More often than not, I would simply immerse myself in the surroundings and, at times, felt as much of part of the landscape as the trees, sky and even rain that I began to take on a feeling of "oneness" with all if it, something that does not happen sitting behind a desk, which is so much a part of my life.

The ride had already taken me through California and Arizona; with about 750 miles under my belt, I reached the Continental Divide, elevation 7,245 feet, which was marked with a modest sign, 50 feet off of Interstate 40 in the middle of nowhere about 25 miles east-southeast from Gallup, New Mexico. There were some dilapidated and abandoned structures nearby, the skeletons of what use to be the Great Divide Trading Company, the Continental Trading Post and Top O' The World Hotel & Café.

Not exactly the place I expected to come across another human being. Just as I was done taking a "selfie" next to the modest 8 x 6-foot marker, a doctor from Pennyslvania riding his Harley Davidson, happened to stop by at the same time. We spoke briefly about our respective journeys, which had us crossing paths going in opposite directions. He acknowledged he was the father of three adult sons so, naturally, I presented him with a Great Dads Coin.

Most of the time when you reach a mountain top, there is a lot of ceremony and celebration. Not here. The entire encounter lasted no more than 15 minutes and we were each back on our journeys.

It's important to understand a bit about this incredible natural line of demarcation and the important role it plays in the ecosystem of the planet, especially here in North America.

The Continental Divide of the Americas, also called the Great Divide, separates the watersheds of the Pacific Ocean from those of the Atlantic and Arctic Oceans. It runs from the Seward Peninsula in Alaska, through western Canada along the crest of the Rocky Mountains, including through Glacier National Park, Yellowstone National Park, and Rocky Mountain National Park, to New Mexico. From there, it follows the crest of Mexico's Sierra Madre Occidental and extends to the tip of South America. It is crossed by the Panama Canal and by the two outlets of Isa Lake in Yellowstone National Park.

Technically a continental divide is a drainage divide on a continent such that the drainage basin on one side of the divide feeds into one ocean or sea, and the basin on the other side either feeds into a different ocean or sea, or else is endorheic, or a closed basin and not connected to the open sea.

That chance encounter has stayed with me ever since, for many reasons, first and foremost is what the "Continental Divide" is really all about. It's basically "the decider" when it comes to the ripple effect in nature that determines growth for everything below it. As I stood at 7,245 feet above sea level, next to the sign that clearly stated "Rainfall divides at this point. To the west, it drains into the Pacific Ocean, to the east, into the Atlantic Ocean."

I could not help but think how many "great divides" I have had as a father when events in my life could push me one way or the other, thus affecting my family and children. Difficulties that were opportunities in disguise for me to become a better father, are sometimes around every turn in the road, much like this ride.

A friend whom, through both circumstance and choice, found himself divorced after a marriage of 25 years, which had produced two really incredible children. He had been a constant presence in their lives from the moment they were born and had built a strong enduring bond with both his daughter and son, a strength that would be needed and tested as the divorce and subsequent changes in family dynamics took effect. There probably isn't any "right time" to divorce (not to say that divorce isn't the right choice for some couples, just that children who are part of that equation take a hit, no matter their age). While his children were both older, one in college and the other in high school, the "continental divide" concept came into play as it does in major life situations. "Rain" in the form of loss of the traditional family structure, two parents that were hurting amid the chaos of the situation, the inevitable upheaval of the physical home and friends along with finances and a million other assorted bits of broken pieces that had been held in place for years, would take a toll on his children. A divorce decree in court is only a piece of paper, the residual effects of divorce cannot be defined in such small and narrow terms. Divorce shakes the very foundation children are accustomed to and experts have called divorce a "water shed event" in life that forever alters their perspective of relationships and communication. The lurid details we hear on the news about celebrity divorce, the over-loaded television channels featuring shows glorifying broken families and the sad aftermath of adults acting out of their worst selves, have become commonplace and all about ratings. The sad truth is certain television shows are making millions of dollars by exploiting a serious problem in our society, one that is responsible for countless relationships broken beyond repair between a father and his children.

With all that (and more in his mind) he knew his actions as their father would determine to a great degree which way the "rain" was going to go, to the *positive* or the *negative* when it came to defining the future relationship he would forge with both his children. My friend, however, knew the time he had spent in his kid's lives was the leverage point, the "ace in the hole," as it were, when it came to the changing landscape of their lives. He did his utmost to not put his kids "in the middle" which happens way to often in divorce, putting children in a position they are not supposed to be in. They are not the cause of a divorce, nor can they be the solution, no matter how old they are. Knowing a marriage is over is one thing, the process of letting it go is another thing, cultivating a healthy, honest and open communication and relationship with children who are thrust into the middle of it all . . . is perhaps the most important thing.

Simple concept, not the easiest thing to do.

If by chance you are in the process of divorce while reading this book, please consider the following statistics.

Half of all American children will witness the breakup of a parent's marriage. Of these, close to half will also see the breakup of a parent's second marriage.

Among the millions of children who have been witness to their parents' divorce, one of every ten will also live through three or more parental marriage breakups.

As pointed out previously, 40% of children growing up in America today are being raised without their fathers.

Of all children born to married parents this year, 50% will experience the divorce of their parents before they reach their 18th birthday.

Teenagers in single-parent families and in blended families are three times more likely to need psychological help within a given year. Compared to children from homes disrupted by death, children from divorced homes have more psychological problems.

A study of children six years after a parental marriage breakup revealed that, even after all that time, these children tended to be "lonely, unhappy, anxious and insecure."

Seventy percent of long-term prison inmates grew up in broken homes.

Children of divorce are four times more likely to report problems with peers and friends than children whose parents have kept their marriages intact. Children of divorce, particularly boys, tend to be more aggressive toward others than those children whose parents did not divorce.

Children of divorced parents are roughly two times more likely to drop out of high school than their peers who benefit from living with parents who stayed married.

To be clear this isn't about whether or not you should get divorced, but it is about knowing the often overlooked ramifications of that decision and taking into account more than just your feelings and perspective on the situation as a parent.

My associate made every conscious effort he could to offset the possible side effects of the divorce including the following.

Don't badmouth your ex in front of your children. Any feelings you have towards your soon-to-be former spouse are best kept from their ears, as tempting as it might be. The harm done by that sort of diatribe is not fair to unload on your kids.

Be consistent in your affection and attention to your kids, it is part of building and maintaining trust, even though the family as they knew it is no longer, but no matter what, you are still there as their father.

It is critical to take action in the midst of so much change. When they are wanting to share their feelings about what is going on, encourage it, don't dismiss it no matter how old they are. My friend is still having an occasional "purge" conversation with his daughter, five years after the divorce was "final." Divorce is like a death of sorts, and it's never about "getting over it" but rather "going through it" at different levels for the rest of your life, and the lives of your children.

No matter who is "right" or "wrong" in the divorce situation, both parents have created it. How you, as a father, treat their mother no matter how your ex-wife might have treated you, will set the tone for the redefinition of your family. That type of behavior will result in respect that will increase over time and surpass the lack of respect that results when pain and hurt rule emotions.

The Continental Divide, that line which determines which way the flow of water will go and the effect it has until it reaches the sea, is something to keep in mind as you make decisions and declarations that will not only affect your life but your children and *their* children as well.

Choose your route wisely.

Ten

The $250k Commitment

"A father is a banker provided by nature."

—French Proverb

If you are by chance the father of an "all knowing, all seeing" teenager, then by now you know two things for certain.

1. Raising a child (or children) can be the most rewarding, frustrating, confusing, enlightening, heart breaking, wonderful, validating, difficult (shall I continue?) undertaking of your life. That undertaking thing is a reference to how many times you have felt "buried" under the responsibility for the health and welfare of your offspring. The word "responsibility" contains one of the hidden secrets of being a 21st Century Dad, which is "the ability to respond." As for all great challenges in life, our response is often more important than the event we are responding to. I am often quoted as asking my kids, "Is that good or bad?" in an effort to help defuse the situation and take a step back before reacting.

2. The second big "Aha" is kids are expensive. I'm speaking from experience, having two kids in college and three who have already graduated from college. But for the sake of this work and to make some salient points (hopefully) along the way, consider this from the United States Department of Agriculture (USDA). If you have a child that was born in 2015, the average total expenditure from the time of their birth to the age of 18 is . . . is . . . wait for it . . . *$250,000.*

Nice chunk of change . . . *Did I mention I have five children?*

There is more good news! The USDA adjusted the amount for inflation that put the figure a bit higher, around $304,000.00 or *the current median price of a two bedroom condo in Chicago.* The price of that piece of real estate is down 1.6% from 2014, but besides the median price and the possible projected investment you are going to make in your kids for nearly two decades being the same amount, one thing is certainly different. The cost of raising your children is not ever, going to go down . . . *only up*.

It's the "$250k Commitment." The cost is per child so you do the math.

Here are how the numbers break down. For a two parent family with a median income between $61,530 and $106,540. The annual cost per child ranges between $12,800 and $14,970 per child, per year-Housing: 30%, Childcare: 18%, Education: 18%" and Food: 16%, which seems low for anyone who has boys knows they can easily eat their way through the rent money if left to their own devices.

Note, these expenses do NOT factor in the costs of college, pregnancy and birth or other expenses after the age of 18. From my own personal experience, out-of-pocket college costs can range from $100k to $400k per child, depending on two vs. four years (or more), public vs. private and based on the geographic proximity to home to cover travel costs.

The hard truth is that for many young, single parents or even young couples, who become parents while still in high school, their parents remain a funding source, an economic back wall. With regard to education, for many kids *their college expense* becomes *their parent's college tuition* all over again as the kids struggle to gain a financial foothold, without anything definite on the horizon to lessen the burden of student loans. I will forgo the lecture, but money is my business and planning ahead will go a long way to easing the burden of the rising cost of education. Unfortunately, just because your kids turn 18 doesn't mean the "Bank of Dad" closes. Many times it's just beginning to open, and you begin to understand that ATM actually means "All The Money."

So on paper, the "$250k Commitment" covers roughly 6,570 days. $38/day/child doesn't seem overwhelming, but multiply by 30 and it's $1,142/month/child. Keep in mind this is the going rate for a traditional family with two parents and two kids and these are 2015 dollars. Factor in inflation and these numbers logically increase over time.

What happens when the economic rug gets pulled out from under a family with a child, due to a job loss, illness, separation or divorce? What about the kids who had no rug to start with due to an absent father from the time of birth? What do they do for 18 years?

At the risk of being redundant, I will simply restate that without some sort of financial safety net under them, these kids have a near impossible task of climbing out of a hole, *they didn't dig*, with very few tools to do so. These are the *at-risk youth*, a term (according to Wikipedia) that came into use after the 1983 article *A Nation at Risk*, published by the National Commission on Excellence in Education. The article described American society as being economically and socially endangered. "At-risk" students are those students who have been labeled, either officially or unofficially, as being in danger of academic failure. In the U.S., each state defines "at-risk" differently, so it is difficult to compare the varying state policies on the subject.

Students who are labeled as "at-risk" face a number of challenges other students do not. According to Becky Smerdon, at the American Institutes for Research, students, especially boys, with low socioeconomic status (and therefore more likely to be labeled "at-risk") show feelings of isolation and estrangement in their schools.

It all comes full circle, as with all things of great importance, it begins and ends at home. Father absence is clearly one of the leading causes of "at-risk youth" in America.

Finding the foundational cause of any pressing issue or challenge is essential to developing a solution. Consider, Americans spend an estimated $3 billion dollars a year maintaining our lawns including weed control. Simply mowing the lawn and cutting off the tops of the weeds is only a stop gap measure, a quick fix which produces a cosmetic effect.

Dandelions, for example, those pesky "weeds" that come in hundreds of species are enemy #1 for lawn lovers across America. Before the advent of weed control chemicals to eradicate such plants, the one way to make sure dandelions did not make a return engagement was to get a bucket, a weed puller and spend some time on your knees digging them out one-by-one by the root. That requires a serious time commitment as well as effort to get at the root of the problem and pull it out. Prior to, or in lieu of, using chemicals, it is the only way to permanently fix the problem of dandelions. Like every other issue in our lives, you have to get to the root cause. It's the only way we are going to make a serious dent in the weeds of father absence, which have taken over the garden of our communities across the country.

While it may (or may not) be a good idea to start digging out dandelions in someone else's yard, there are things we can each do as fathers and father figures to get at the root cause of a kid who doesn't have a father in his or her life.

Becoming a mentor, especially once your kids are older, is a great way to leverage your experiences for the benefit of others. You've developed a treasure trove of experiences, events and lessons learned as a father. The massive resources you have gathered and the incredible amount of time, energy and effort you have put in to become the best father you can be are worthy of your reinvestment.

To let all that experience go to waste simply because your kids are "on their own" (*and are they really ever on their own? I'll get to that in a moment*) diminishes the sacred contract you signed when you became that guy called "Dad."

Your expertise, compassion, leadership and strength are needed desperately in the lives of young men and women who have no idea what it really means to have a man, a father, in their life who will be there and bring The Quadrant (*spiritually, emotionally, physically* and *emotionally*) to the forefront of their lives.

We deal with bottom lines all the time in business, and this is as good a place as any to insert a "here's the bottom line" thought.

The bottom line is a 21ˢᵗ Century Dad understands *they are all our kids in some way, shape or form.*

The kid you mentor now, at a young age, might make the decision later in life to not do drugs, steal, cheat, lie or commit crimes or suicide. Your *presence and voice* are that important.

There are resources in the back of this book that will support you should you chose to put your cape on and show a kid how to leap over the gap of father absence in his or her life, stop the locomotive of despair in its tracks and find the superhero who lives within them.

This chapter began by shedding light on the expense associated with being a parent, at least the numbers as published for the first 18 years. The cost to our society when dads are not present or responsible is off the charts. Incarceration costs on average $31,286 per prisoner/year and the aggregate total of 40 states that participated in the 2012 Vera Institute of Justice survey comes to a staggering $68 billion dollars. Add in the amount from the 10 states that did not participate and it balloons to an estimated $75 billion dollars.

There is one more concept for you to consider when it comes to the financial pillar of fatherhood.

For many of you reading this-born between 1946 and 1964-(and that includes me), we are called "Baby Boomers."

Enter a new species of young person called "Boomerang Children." These are the offspring who "leave the nest," try to fly for a time and end up returning home, battered, bruised and not only looking for their old room to recuperate and "figure it out" but also, according to a 2010 study done by Charles Schwab called "Families and Money," are needing some ongoing financial support. The Schwab survey found that among parents of 23-to-28-year-olds, 41% continue to financially support their children on some level.

And you thought at 18 they were out the door, on their own and all was right with the world!

Maybe that's how it was when you grew up, but the rules have changed due to many factors not the least of which, unfortunately, is a sense of "entitlement" that one in three parents say the "20-somethings" have that was devoid in previous generations. The big kicker . . . nearly 64% of parents in the survey felt their kids are not worried in the least about being a financial burden on them.

Learned behavior? Overspending? The "What's In It For Me" generation? The rising cost of making your way in the world? Whatever the cause, the financial support you give as a father can at times be a very thin line. Even if you end up reverting your kid's room from the den you couldn't wait to build back to a bedroom, the support is important on so many levels. Having an understanding of what you can do, and should do, when it comes to "being there" for your kids financially is always a teachable moment.

Being there for them doesn't always mean opening your wallet, but also your heart and mind to the situation and acting accordingly.

So here is what we know.

According to the experts, the surveys and the numbers, you signed up for the "$250k Commitment" the moment you became a father and for the next 18 years of your child's life. Anticipate "The Bank of Dad" will be called on for more withdrawals than deposits. There are, of course, variations on that theme, but the bottom line (*again*) is it's a far different world than even a decade ago. Being a dad in the 21st century means it's okay to have the same old tool box but with some brand new tools as part of the inventory, which means extra cash on hand in your wallet and maybe stuffed under the mattress.

You're going to need it, and it's part of the deal.

Just make sure it's not the mattress in your kid's bedroom that used to be the den, they might be back sooner than you think. It's better to be prepared to act and not have to, than have to act and not be prepared. No more is that true than when it comes to The Quarter Million Dollar Commitment.

Are you ready?

Eleven
Let's Shake on It

I cannot think of any need in childhood as strong as the need for a father's protection.
—Sigmund Freud

I've lost count of the many people I met on the ride. Some for just a few moments while others were much longer encounters. As I think back on it all, there were so many faces and places that made up the mosaic of the Dads Honor Ride experience. Once people found out about our mission, their words of encouragement became extra fuel of sorts, a reserve tank if you will, when my legs or mind began to fatigue. Toots on a horn, waves from passersby or even the occasional thumbs up all help pushed me forward. There was nothing more heartening, intimate or strengthening than a firm handshake accompanied by eye-to eye-contact.

It was even more impactful if there was a Great Dads Coin (GDC) in one hand, being given as a gift of recognition, a tangible reminder of our encounter. More about that in a bit.

As far back as the fifth century BC, humans have extended a hand to one another. This simple ritual was confirmation of peace and a sign no weapon was being hidden in the hand. More recently, the traditional handshake was broadened to include the popular "fist bump." Some insist the great baseball player Stan Musial was the originator back in the 1950s as a way to avoid picking up germs from teammates.

While I can understand Stan "The Man" being concerned about hygiene, I have no such reservations or concerns about making contact. I'm more focused on the energy and intent of who I am with when shaking hands.

A slew of memories come flooding back, when I think about extending my hand to so many incredible people along the Mother Road.

Like the grandmother who saw us on the evening news in Oklahoma then tracked us down to make a $100 donation to "the cause," and wanted to share her story about being a single mom. There was a gathering of "dads at the diner" also in the "Sooner State." Connecting with Jasmine, our waitress in Tulsa at "Pizza Express," who told me an incredible story about the positive influence of her stepfather. Being interviewed by Kim Tobin, the early morning news anchor at NBC4 in Albuquerque and Police Office Pedro Martinez in Amarillo, Texas.

We made connections with more than a dozen dads at the Midpoint Café and Gift Shop on historic Route 66. This little out of the way diner in Adrian, Texas, is located about 50 miles west of Amarillo. The diner's claim to fame is that it is located exactly 1,139 miles from Los Angeles and 1,139 miles from Chicago.

At the official midpoint along Route 66 in Adrian, Texas, with young Dave.
1,139 Miles to Los Angeles and 1,139 miles to Chicago.

There were retirees traveling with their spouses from east to west and west to east. There was a group of young biker fathers from Austria & Sweden riding their rented BMW motorcycles from Chicago to LA.

The highlight of our stop in Adrian was meeting Mike Cruz, a 68-year-old retired engineer from San Diego. Mike was riding the entire Route 66 solo. His bicycle was loaded down with four saddle bags and he was pulling a small trailer with a tent and a small cache of bike parts. He was making the 2,448-mile journey at a pace of 50 miles a day and 10 miles per hour. Pretty darn impressive. After buying this road warrior lunch, we shook hands as I slipped him a Great Dads Coin, and agreed to reconnect when he made it to Chicago three weeks later.

The most memorable of all handshakes was with Tim Parker (who I mentioned earlier), the former Marine in Prescott, Arizona, who is the executive director of the Set Free Center, a drug and alcohol program serving 4,000 youth annually. After presenting him with a Great Dads Coin, he turned around and presented me with The Whole Armor Of God coin. I will not soon forget the prayers Tim offered me, Addie and Wilk, the four of us in a circle, standing shoulder to shoulder in downtown Prescott. The energy was palpable. In fact, I've carried that Whole Armor Of God coin with me every day since then, putting it in my pocket with the constancy of putting on your seatbelt when you get in your car. It also brings to mind the old American Express commercial with the tagline: "Don't leave home without it."

I have presented hundreds of Great Dads Coins while on the Dads Honor Ride and during the past few years. Many of the names have long since faded from my memory. What each handshake, whether firm or weak, sweaty, cold or trembling represents is the opportunity to connect with men on a personal level, as dads, one on one.

I have also had the privilege of presenting Great Dad Coins (in no particular order of importance) to: entertainer Usher, actors Gary Sinise and Joe Mantegna, basketball's Dwayne Wade, author Stedman Graham, Allen Lynch (U.S. Congressional Medal of Honor recipient) and comedian Tom Dreesen. A few other names just to round out the short list include NFL Hall of Famers Mike Singletary and Richard Dent, General Ray Odierno, U.S Army (Ret.) and Former President Bill Clinton.

All these men (and hundreds more) extended their hand as I did to them, and I was able to transfer a coin for the dedication to the duty of fatherhood. Most were deeply touched by the gesture.

Because it's not just a coin with some words and images.

The "Great Dads Coin" is in my opinion the most important coin a father can have in his pocket, a constant reminder of the importance of the role he has accepted. I created the GDC based in part on the concept of "the military challenge coin" which has an incredible history of honoring men.

Air warfare was a new phenomenon during World War I. When the Army created flying squadrons they were manned with volunteer pilots from every walk of civilian life. While some of the early pilots came from working class or rural backgrounds, many were wealthy college students who withdrew from classes in the middle of the year, drawn by the adventure and romance of the new form of warfare.

As the legend goes, one such student, a wealthy lieutenant, ordered small, solid-bronze medallions (or coins) struck, which he then presented to the other pilots in his squadron as mementos of their service together. The coin was gold-plated, bore the squadron's insignia, and was quite valuable. One of the pilots in the squadron, who had never owned anything like the coin, placed it in a leather pouch he wore around his neck for safekeeping. A short while later, this pilot's aircraft was heavily damaged by ground fire (other sources claim it was an aerial dogfight), forcing him to land behind enemy lines, resulting in his capture by the Germans. The Germans confiscated the personal belongings from his pockets, but they didn't catch the leather pouch around his neck. On his way to a permanent prisoner of war facility, he was held overnight in a small German-held French village near the front. During the night, the town was bombarded by the British, creating enough confusion to allow the pilot to escape.

The pilot avoided German patrols by donning civilian attire, but all of his identification had been confiscated so he had no way to prove his identity. With great difficulty, he crept across no-man's land and made contact with a French patrol. Unfortunately for him, the French had been on the lookout for German saboteurs dressed as civilians. The French mistook the American pilot for a German saboteur and immediately prepared to execute him.

Desperate to prove his allegiance and without any identification, the pilot pulled out the coin from his leather pouch and showed it to his French captors. One of the Frenchmen recognized the unit insignia on the coin and delayed the execution long enough to confirm the pilot's identity.

I was vaguely familiar with the history of challenge coins and had received a handful of them from retiring military friends and some nonprofits who had used them to commemorate their anniversary. One such coin was in celebration of the 150-year anniversary of the creation of the U.S. Congressional Medal of Honor. Thirty-three Medal of Honor recipients were present at the dinner and each of the honorees and the guests, including myself, received a 150-year anniversary coin.

With all that in mind, I searched the Internet for a dads coin, but couldn't find one. So, I was inspired to create a coin to be used as a gift to honor fathers, grandfathers, stepfathers and father-figures.

Every design element of the GDC has a purpose and meaning for what it means to be a great dad.

The circle is an ancient and universal symbol of unity. The outer ring has a continual chain link design symbolizing the everlasting and interlocking connection a father shares with his child. On the face and around the perimeter are the core values every Great Dad possesses: Love, Honesty, Patience and Commitment. The numbers 2-4-7-3-6-5 represent the daily, weekly, and year-long commitment Great Dads make. The bald eagle represents protection and guardianship. The banner includes the phrase "magna pater," which is Latin for Great Dad. In the center is the heart, the universal symbol of love.

On the reverse side and around the perimeter is the phrase "Great Dads Are Present Physically, Emotionally and Spiritually." While society puts a high price tag on dads supporting their children financially, it's equally important for dads to have a meaningful physical, emotional and spiritual presence in their children's lives. This treasured keepsake can be carried around daily or proudly displayed at home or work.

The physical coin itself is also the reminder of the financial component of fatherhood because, true to form, your kids might be in your pockets for a long time in more ways than one.

So the Dads Honor Ride was at times a bit like the early days of the stagecoach, thundering across the dusty west, closely guarding strong boxes full of coins in-between banks and towns. The difference, of course, is that I wasn't holding onto these valuable tokens, but doling them out to dads from all different walks of life.

In a handshake . . . *not* a fist bump.

Passing along this coin has made me even more aware of the concept of the "ripple effect" as it pertains to fatherhood. The lives dads lead in the 21st century are far different in many ways than just one generation ago, when social media might have meant a bar stool and Amazon was still just a really big river. I have heard over and over how the coins have helped men think more consciously and subconsciously about their role as father. A quick glance at the coin among the quarters, nickels and dimes can prompt a thought to make a call, send a text or simply follow through on a promise. Some mention the GDC has a way of bringing them back to "center" with their actions then rippling out to their children with some sense of consciousness and intent. With the ongoing battle for our time with business meetings, deadlines and details, it's so easy to forget, get busy, or be distracted from our role as dads.

For that reason the GDC has a far greater value than any other coin. It's value only *increases* over time the more it gets used, it's never stagnant nor does it decrease in value just because your kids have become young adults.

One of the great things about biking 2,300 *plus* miles is the time to recall the many encounters I have had about this mission I am on, and how that coin has become a conduit for conversations that might not have taken place any other way.

I can remember having lunch in Milwaukee with friend Shawn Wilson, who at the time was the first President and CEO of The New Look Foundation created by the performing artist, Usher. We were discussing the many facets of fatherhood. I had presented Shawn with a Great Dads Coin on a previous trip to Atlanta. As we were having lunch, he shared with me that he keeps his coin close by, especially when traveling, making it a little less difficult to maintain a connection with his kids. Even though Shawn is an outstanding father and role model, he understands the value in having a reminder. He shared with me how he has passed along coins to a myriad of friends and associates who have responded in many different ways. Out of the 30 or 40 coins Shawn gave out, it sparked a deep dialogue with more than a few of the dads, which in turn gives each of them an opportunity to have that dialogue with other dads and a further ripple effect.

"Commitment, Love, Honesty, Patience 24/7/365."

Every month I have the opportunity to present coins to men in many different situations. I always present the coin in a sacred handshake that usually starts with "Thank you for being a great dad to your child and for being a role model to countless others." During some of those exchanges, I can often feel through that handshake a physical vibration, something striking an emotional cord, brought to life by the simple gesture of a handshake. The GDC is simply tangible evidence of our relationship with one another, whether from dad to dad or child to father.

To jump back a moment to the concept of the military challenge coin I referred to earlier, here is the conclusion to that story. Once the pilot safely returned to his squadron, it became a tradition for all members to carry their coin at all times. To ensure compliance, the pilots would challenge each other to produce the coin. If the person being challenged couldn't produce the coin, he was required to buy a drink of choice for the challenger; if the challenged could produce the coin, the challenger would purchase the drink.

If by chance we cross paths, and I can extend my hand to you, passing along with it a GDC, it's up to you to carry it from then on. If by chance we meet again down the road and I challenge you to show your coin to me, and you don't have it . . . you have to buy me a drink. To be fair, if I left mine on the dresser that day, and you ask me for mine . . . in the tradition of the great aviators of yesterday, I'm buying. Let's take that one step further. Even if we've never met, if you challenge me to produce my GDC and I don't have it, I'm buying.

Twelve
Obi Dad Kenobi

Do. Or do not. There is no try.

—Yoda

Zipping along the western half of the United States on my two-wheeled time machine, wearing a tear drop-shaped helmet, dark wrap-around glasses protecting my eyes and a sleek skin-tight outfit to cut down on the drag, one might think I resembled a futuristic pilot of sorts, slicing through halls of air, in a galaxy not too far away. While not quite at "light" speed, I kept a respectable pace, averaging 14–17 mph on most days.

Although at times I might look like a sci-fi figure wheeling my way down the asphalt, I would never be confused with a "Jedi." Admittedly, I am not very well steeped in the "Star Wars Nation." I know enough about the films to understand there is a lesson in fatherhood and mentoring buried within the films. I am reminded of the one of the oldest and most powerful of "Jedi Masters" who is talking in his sing-song way about the young Luke Skywalker who just can't seem to get the hang of becoming a Jedi Knight.

Yoda, the ancient one, says out loud into the void of the swamps of the Dagobah system "I cannot teach him, the boy has no patience."

The distended, looming voice of Obi Wan Kenobi responds to his friend with "He will learn patience" to which Yoda replies, "Hmm. Much anger in him like his father."

The "ghost" of Obi Wan, who died off in *Star Wars Episode IV: A New Hope* (after being eliminated by Luke's father Darth Vader), answers with "Was I any different when you taught me?"

That short exchange from the blockbuster *The Empire Strikes Back* reminds me of the deep importance of having a "master mentor" of sorts when it comes to the "Force of Fatherhood" and navigating all the galaxies, evil overlords, lightsabers and strange doings, which are a part of each day as "Dad."

Obi Wan Kenobi was young master Luke's first mentor, a guiding hand to show him what lies dormant within, how to access it and bring it forth to be a positive *force* in the universe.

But first a short trip in the "way-back-when machine."

Times have changed from when "Dad" would sit outside of the delivery room door waiting to hand out cigars to his buddies, with a blue band for a boy and pink one for a girl. Offering maybe a wave or two through the glass window as a nurse held up the new arrival, and then the eventual trip home to show off the babe to adoring neighbors and family. More than likely, Dad was back to work, "bringing home the bacon" and Mom took care of diapers, feedings and all the connected duties that a newborn might need.

For the most part, those days are gone, never to return again. It's a whole new universe.

California was the first state to institute paid family leave, at a portion of your salary for up to six weeks. Rhode Island and New Jersey followed suit with similar laws. These days, 21ˢᵗ Century Dads are far more apt to take sick leave or vacation days to have "bonding time" with their children. There are numerous websites you can visit that will give you a check list of options in your area, if that is something in your future, (*you know* . . . *babies*). Mothers, of course, are already connected to the life inside them for nearly a year, and as dads we have some catching up to do.

Matter of fact, researchers are looking deep inside the "brain of dad" for more clues on the critical importance of a father getting "connected" to his children as soon as possible. Trials with the Degu rat (a species that is known to be "biparental" sharing the duties of raising their pups, much like humans) populations show that even at the level of a rodent, the absence of a father creates a true and significant emotional and social void in the pups just as it would in a human family. When Poppa Degu stuck around and remained with his brood, their brains developed normally. Conversely when Pops was removed from the nest shortly after birth, the pups "synapses" or information centers in their brains began to break down significantly.

The moral of the story is simply this . . . *if you are going to be a rat* . . . be like the Degu. In the whole of the animal kingdom (which includes you and me) the bonding of the father to his offspring is a crucial element in the well-being of that child or pup or any other life form.

But how do you create the bond if you didn't grow up with that sort of connection to your own father? Well . . . Luke Skywalker (who had an absent father) didn't know a lightsaber from a flashlight until Obi Wan Kenobi showed up.

You need to find your own *Obi Dad Kenobi*, a master mentor, a veteran who has been around for a while, raised his own children and has that "connection" with them, not just in words but in deeds. In case you cannot think of someone, I have a guy you should know about.

His name is Greg Bishop.

"My six brothers and I grew up taking care of babies, which happens when your parents have 13 kids. To us boys, babies were like puppies; while a lot of work at times, they were fun to play with," recalls Greg. "They made great amateur wrestlers and you could always make them happy by the time Mom got home.

"When my first child arrived," Greg continued, "I was a natural at calming him when he cried and, of course, making him happy. After four kids, other guys were asking me for advice, so I decided to help. It's nice to be good at something important.

"In 1990, I recruited a few friends and asked them to bring their babies to the local hospital to show the ropes to some dads-to-be. When a few 'rookies' said they had never held a baby before, we handed them ours and they went home thinking, 'I can do this.' They did, and later returned as 'veterans' with their own babies to guide the next batch of rookies, and *Boot Camp for New Dads* was off and running.

At Springfield, Missouri, Boot Camp for New Dads Program.
Left to right: David Hirsch, CK Wright and Patrick Wierzchucki

"No women over two feet tall were allowed; just babies and men. No question was stupid, no topic off-limits, like a 'nursery in a locker room.'"

Boot Camp for New Dads now operates across the United States, on U.S. military bases in Japan and Italy and in the U.K. and Canada. That small group of guys in 1990 has turned into more than 350,000 men prepared to be fathers.

In the past 26 years since he created the concept, Greg also established "Dads Adventure" in 1995 to sponsor the nonprofit boot camp and develop broad support for new fathers.

All this great and valuable information is literally at your fingertips online where you can find out more about Greg's superb programs, articles, videos and the powerful "Ask A Dad" option that has 300 versions of *Obi Dad Kenobi* waiting to help you navigate the vast universe that awaits new fathers. If you are a seasoned pro, there is an opportunity to become a mentor as well and pass along your knowledge to the next generation of fathers. You can connect with "Boot Camp For New Dads" in the resource section of this book.

So *you are not alone* when it comes to stepping up to the opportunity *and* responsibility of fatherhood.

Back to Luke Skywalker who had some serious "absent father issues" to the utmost degree (and without getting all Maury Povich deep on this and doing a paternity test) it turns out that Luke has been wondering who his dad is all these years and searching for his own identity.

Eventually, with the help of Obi Wan Kenobi, Luke discovers to his great disappointment who is father *really is* and, of course, the evil Lord Darth Vader (not exactly the best role model) dispatches Skywalker's mentor . . . even though some think Obi Wan just changed form and continued on in another realm.

Not going to speculate on that.

Then along comes the aforementioned Yoda who, compared to Obi Wan Kenobi's more "Zen like" delivery on life lessons, is a bit tougher on the kid as a mentor, more demanding and decisive along with speaking in a strange "object-subject-verb" word order as discussed by an academic group of syntacticians (those who study linguistic syntax-now that is deep.)

Yoda's message is clear.

"The Force is with you when you find the Source within you."

Finding your spiritual center as a father and as a man, takes a mentor, someone who has experience in lightsabers, diapers, bullying by other kids, losing teeth, first dates, last dates, sex, money, rock and roll and how to try and go to sleep the first time your kid uses the car and breaks curfew. They are the tests that come with fatherhood that we have to get a passing grade on in order to share our experiences and journey with the next generation of dads, supporting and enabling them to rise above, and go beyond, previous definitions of fatherhood.

The word "mentor" comes from the character of the same name in Homer's *Odyssey* and means "wise adviser." Even though at times, Mentor was ineffective as a voice of reason until the goddess Athena took on the old man's appearance in order to guide young Telemachus (who was a figure in Greek mythology and the son of Odysseus and Penelope) through his difficult times. The first four books of the *Odyssey* focus on Telemachus' journeys in search of news about his father, who has yet to return home from the Trojan War.

Another son looking for his dad.

It's easy to get caught up in theory-based living with the pace we all keep. If all I did was blueprint, discuss and dream about the Dads Honor Ride but never put my butt on the bike, I would have missed experiences of a lifetime, many of which are shared in this book.

Same rule applies when it comes to being a father, you need a mentor, a wise adviser or a shoulder to lean on and an ear to listen, just like Obi Wan Kenobi, Greg Bishop and Yoda.

Thirteen
Identity

Allow yourself to be a beginner. No one starts off being excellent.

—Unknown

So there we were in Wickenburg, Arizona. We had just finished day three of the ride. After a long hot shower, Wilk, Addie and I headed out to dinner to with my friend Albert Pooley. He is the founder of the Native American Fatherhood & Families Association (NAFFA) located in Mesa, Arizona. NAFFA provides dads on a third of the 600 reservations in North America with resources on how to rebuild relationships with their families. Albert brought a guest to dinner, a young Native American father by the name of Shawn Taylor. Shawn had gone through the Fatherhood Is Sacred® program and was now working for NAFFA.

By the end of the dinner, Shawn asked if he could join us on the ride the next day. I was a little reluctant to say yes for two reasons. First, because each registered rider was required to raise money. Secondly, and let me be perfectly honest, Shawn is probably 5'7" and weighs close to 275 pounds. He certainly didn't fit the image of an endurance bike rider. After all, we were putting in 100+ mile days and the last thing we needed was someone who was going to be slowing us down, or God forbid, who might get injured due to inexperience or lack of proper preparation. While I was impressed with his interest, I didn't want to offer any encouragement. Sometimes I'm too polite and not overly confrontational, so we just left it open ended.

When we parted after dinner, Albert and I discussed meeting in Flagstaff around noon the next day to do a TV interview. He told me he would talk with Shawn and I thought that was the end of it. The next day we made it up to Flagstaff, which was a pretty challenging trek. As planned we rendezvoused at Flagstaff Medical Center to talk with the media about Boot Camp for New Dads and NAFFA.

Much to our surprise there was Shawn, duffle bag in-hand, and apparently ready to start riding with us. I was still pretty skeptical about his abilities on a bike for such a distance. After a tasty lunch at Altitude's Bar

& Grill, Shawn and I suited up for the approaching rain and headed toward Winslow, Arizona, for the 58-mile journey east.

Our agreement was, for whatever reason, if he wasn't able to keep pace he'd have to get in one of the support vehicles. We rode together for 10–15 miles and then I didn't see him for quite awhile as I needed to hit my pace to keep in line with our time frame. Long story short, he made it all the way to Albuquerque, a distance of 325 miles during the next two and a half days.

So my first big "aha" was that I had unfairly judged this heavy set guy who hadn't trained but was able to persevere. While he didn't ride every one of those 325 miles, he did a very respectful job keeping up for a rookie. Ultimately, we decided for financial reasons, (since he hadn't done any fundraising) we couldn't justify the $125/day it was costing us to keep him on. We parted ways on friendly terms and he found a ride back to Mesa.

I learned later he would have gone all the way to Chicago, if we would have let him. With the benefit of hindsight, I'm glad we let him tag along, because he taught each of us a valuable lesson about not being judgmental. It was a good reminder not to judge a book by its cover. He had an inner drive and passion I could not measure to be part of the Honor Ride. I am sure once he got on the bike, he too had some serious concerns to overcome in his own abilities, but he cast them aside and kept pedaling. He also helped underscore the importance of being fiscally responsible. Dads Honor Ride is a fundraiser and the riders needed to raise more than they cost.

As I was riding the next day from Albuquerque to Santa Rosa, New Mexico, I started thinking about all the people who were offering their words of caution to me about doing the ride. Who did I think I was at 54, with almost no endurance bike riding experience, to believe I could ride 2,300+ miles in 21 days? I remember very distinctly meeting, just weeks before the ride, with one of my former business associates who has a very high level job at City Hall. He told me flat out "don't waste your time and all the money involved. It's just not going to happen. It's going to end poorly and you're going to be very embarrassed." I'm glad I didn't heed his advice, another lesson learned.

As George Bernard Shaw said, "People who say something cannot be done, should never interrupt those who are doing it." This is a great reminder as fathers. We need to be very deliberate about how we encourage or discourage our kids. In all cases, except where safety is an issue, I've tried to err on the side of being encouraging. Better to take a risk and fail than to never have tried.

Some people are more vain than others, but at some level we are all consciously or subconsciously concerned about our identity. For good or bad, most men achieve their identity from the work we do. Think of a social setting where guys are exchanging business cards and someone in the group is unemployed. He has no card to exchange. It's as if he is somehow not worth as much, at least at that point in time, as his peers.

Men are strange creatures in that regard. Why is it that so much of our identity is tied to our title or position in a company? There is a great danger in getting your identity intertwined with your career, because then if you lose your work, you lose yourself. Who you *are* is not what you *do*. It is a painful lesson to learn, especially for men, who have a higher than normal mortality rate within the first five years after retirement as they struggle to find their identity after years of being defined by what they do.

I'm just as guilty, at times, of passing judgment about people (like I did with Shawn). We make intuitive or gut decisions about people because of their height, their weight, the color of their skin, their IQ, the type of clothes they wear, the car they drive, and the list goes on and on. In some cases, our first impression is an accurate one, but all too often when you get to know someone your opinion is different.

Stedman Graham, one of my good friends and someone who I've spared with on the tennis courts, wrote an impressive book a few years ago entitled *Identity, Your Passport to Success*. In it, Steadman shares very openly what it was like growing up as an African American youth in Whitesboro, New Jersey, a small black community surrounded by a predominantly white community. As he tells the story, the catch phrase was "Nothing good ever comes out of Whitesboro." He describes growing up with two disabled brothers and being teased and discriminated against. When he was of college age, he was 6'6" and was labeled a basketball player because of his height.

Years later he realized his struggle wasn't about race but rather "identity." After serving time in the U.S. Army and working in the prison system, he came to see what happens to those who don't have a healthy identity or a process for success. He admits he didn't know who he really was and didn't have a process for becoming successful. Years later he faced a different issue, being labeled as "Oprah's boyfriend." His book and his nine-step program is worth the price and worthy of your time.

It became obvious that while I had made some snap judgments about Shawn, he *knew* himself and what he wanted to achieve better than I ever could. Whatever impetus drove him to connect with me and push himself for 325 miles, comes from an inner knowing of his identity, one I could not see clearly upon first (or even second) glance.

As a father, there is almost no line between who we used to be B.K. (Before Kids) and A.K. (After Kids) as our former selves become blended so closely with the title "dad," it's easy to forget we, too, have to find and retain our identity past the label (impressive and important as it is).

In some ways I suppose it's a bit like Superman, you know . . . Clark Kent . . . mild mannered reporter for a great metropolitan newspaper. On the surface, he is his job, totally engrossed in being the journalist, digging for stories. But underneath that work exterior, there is a big "S" on his chest. This is truly who he is. Only under the most challenging of circumstances does he dash into a phone booth to exchange his *exterior self* for his *interior self*, wherein lies his true power.

I often have wondered if Shawn's children would ever know of their dad's willingness to participate, his courage in taking the risk and ability to push back on his own fears to be part of the Dads Honor Ride. All the traits he displayed in that 325-mile journey are the things that will make him a great father. While I never was able to catch Shawn wearing a cape, it's obvious his true identity was far greater than expected.

Fourteen
Trail of Tears

"Life is a journey, not a destination."
—Ralph Waldo Emerson

The physical aspects of riding over 100 miles most days on the Dads Honor Ride is something that my body adapted to on the road, It's what I had trained for prior to the "launch date" of June 1, 2015. All the best preparations had been made in regards to equipment, support systems and the like. As with any journey of this magnitude, we did the best we could to cover as many bases as possible.

Even with careful planning there were bound to be setbacks and delays, route changes, weather to wait out and speed bumps in many different forms. What I couldn't possibly be prepared for was the deep lessons that awaited me in some of the most unexpected places and the profound impact they had on me at the time and still resonate today.

We were on day 16 traveling from Joplin to Lebanon, Missouri. It had been a day of highs and lows. Not only did we have at least one flat tire, I learned by radio that while attempting a three-point turn in the RV, the crew—no, it was actually Wilk who was driving—had accidently grounded the RV in a ditch. It had taken hours to resolve the situation and they were 30 miles behind and we were essentially out of hydration and not 100% sure we were on the right route. While we were trying to figure out the correct coordinates and best plan of action, I noticed a 10-foot-high federal road sign with the message "Trail of Tears Original Route Next Two Miles" clearly posted. There was nothing in proximity to the sign that would indicate there were any sites to be seen or other historical information in the rather remote, somewhat desolate, non-descript rural area.

I suddenly forgot about all that was going on with the support team and couldn't help thinking about that sign. It got the wheels in my mind spinning at a high revolution. I had some knowledge of "The Trail of Tears" but only a surface understanding from books and articles. Now I was literally riding in the same area where thousands of Native Americans had perished while being forced to march west as part of the Indian Removal Act of 1830. What must have it been like to be one of those dads marching across the country with their family and, in too many cases, watching them perish along the route back in 1838?

President Andrew Jackson had initiated the forced relocation of many Indian Nations from their homelands in the Southeastern United States and they were made to march west in a series of moves that took place over a period of 20 years. Many were held in prison camps awaiting their fate. According to the Cherokee Nation Cultural Resource Center, under orders from President Jackson, the U.S. Army began enforcement of the Removal Act. In 1838, an estimated 20,000 Cherokee walked westward, at gunpoint in some of the worst winter weather you could possibly imagine—rags on their feet, scarce food supplies and maybe a blanket to shield them from the fierce, freezing winds. An estimated *4,000 died* from hunger, exposure and disease.

The journey became a cultural memory as the "trail where they cried" for the Cherokees and other removed tribes. Today it is widely remembered by the general public as the "Trail of Tears." The Oklahoma chapter of the Trail of Tears Association has begun the task of marking the graves of known Trail survivors with a bronze plaque on the headstones.

My mind raced further. What, if anything, had the men, women and children done to warrant such an action outside of being Native American? What would life be like at the end of the trail? How did those who survived the march come back to life? Did they lose their traditions and faith? What twisted logic would cause the government to move this mass of humanity across the country? The consequence, although perhaps unintended, resulted in nearly obliterating an entire segment of American society.

That Trail of Tears sign also got me thinking of some of the experiences I shared as a Kellogg Fellow in my mid-30s. Three of the 50 fellows, in Group 13 of the W.K. Kellogg Foundation national fellows program, were Native Americans. The friendships formed over the three years of the fellowship provided our diverse group of 20- and 30-something-year-old leaders with invaluable insights and experiences. The old saying about not knowing someone until you've walked in their shoes or, in this case, their moccasins, applies.

Informally, the fellowship also included some civility lessons and sensitivity training. One evening we were talking about upward career movement and I recall making some passing remark about starting at the bottom and working your way to higher levels of responsibility. Actually, what I had said was "you have to start out as the low man on the totem pole." You would have thought I had made a hostile statement or used the "N" word. It's a simple phrase that so many of us have uttered with no malice, but what followed was a very condensed lesson about Native American history directed at me in a not so pleasant tone. It was humbling and a bit embarrassing to get schooled in that manner. But it was an important reminder that the wrongs of the past can have an incalculable number of generational ripple effects.

It bears mentioning in this chapter that Native American youth in the 21st century face enormous challenges and the statistics are sad and staggering among the recognized tribes in the United States. Fully 25% of Native American children live in poverty, which is much higher than the national average. They graduate from high school at a rate 17% lower than the national average and their substance abuse and alcohol related incidences are considerably higher. And their exposure to abuse and neglect has been compared in some studies as causing the same symptoms of PTSD as soldiers returning from Afghanistan.

They are twice as likely as any another other race of people in America to die before the age of 24. Suicide rates are many times higher among Native American youth as they struggle with more challenges than the average young person can ever imagine.

There is a direct tie in to all these debilitating statistics as the agony on many reservations goes back past the "Trail of Tears" to the "Trail of Broken Promises" that were given by the government as far back as the early 19th century, but they never received the promised health care, education and housing. Once they had been relocated, they were largely forgotten and have been ever since. The long chain of despair, depression and oppression for the Native American has many links in it, and while the future for so many of these children from homes without fathers is bleak at best, in the midst of such darkness there is a shining light.

Standing on that sacred ground, waiting for my team to catch up, my mind immediately reverted back to the conversations I had with my friend Albert Pooley back on day three when we were in Wickenburg, Arizona. As I mentioned, he is the founder of the Native American Fatherhood & Families Association (NAFFA) located in Mesa, Arizona. NAFFA provides dads on a third of the 600 reservations in North America with resources on how to rebuild relationships with their families. Al and I have been friends for years and his passion is shoring up the sad state of fathering in the lives of Native Americans.

Albert was born to both the Hopi and Navajo Native American cultures. He grew up close to both cultures on the reservation where the love of a father taught him outstanding life lessons. He has taken up the mantle of fatherhood mentoring for a population in dire need of the four elements of The Quadrant (spiritually, emotionally, physically and financially) and while it is a daunting task to say the least, with a Masters of Social Work (MSW) and Masters of Public Administration (MPA), he is equipped on many levels for the challenge.

Albert's mantra is simple and straightforward: "The family is at the heart of the Native American cultures. There is no other work more important than fatherhood and motherhood."

The Mission Statement of NAFFA is just as clear. "To strengthen families by responsibly involving fathers in the lives of their children, families and communities and partnering with mothers to provide happy and safe families." The word *vision* might be defined as "that which you can see in your mind that becomes a guiding force in your life." The Vision Statement that guides Albert and his dedicated staff and over 600 volunteers in programs that span the width of America, from Maine to Hawaii, Alaska to Florida and even past the northern border of the United States into Canada is clear: "Native American Fathers and Mothers as models of healthy parenting for happy and safe families everywhere.

The influence of a loving, caring father in Albert's life became the catalyst for the creation of a foundation that has changed the lives of over 20,000 fathers and mothers (with little or no assistance from federal or state funds) for their programs. Many people and agencies view fathers as the cause of most family and social problems. However, NAFFA takes the position that fathers are not the problem, *but the solution* and must take the lead in keeping families together.

What a concept, one that is built on the following approach based on a culturally rich model that inspires and self-motivates through natural techniques. They help parents devote their best efforts in teaching and raising their children to develop the potential and attributes needed for success in life. Their method is to uplift, encourage, assist and teach. Filling life with hope, gratitude and understanding has a powerful effect in changing attitudes and behavior.

Albert and his team have proven *that there is no better way.*

It is a foundational approach to a fundamental problem, creating and restoring the bond between fathers and their children, strengthening families from within, no matter how much they may go without in terms of material things.

As has been pointed out many times over, (with good reason, because that which we repeat becomes habit for better or for worse, especially when it comes to fatherhood) there is always a choice to be made. To "step up" or "step back" when it comes to being the leader that is needed in our kids' lives. There are always opposing forces at work within each of us but knowing which source to connect with will be your rudder not just as a father, but also as a better human being.

As my radio crackled and the RV made its way to my location, with needed provisions, I remembered an old story that has a few different versions from the Cherokee tradition that goes like this.

A Cherokee Elder is teaching his grandson about life:

"A fight is going on inside me," he said to the boy. "It is a terrible fight and it is between two wolves. One is evil—he is anger, envy, sorrow, regret, greed, arrogance, self-pity, guilt, resentment, inferiority, lies, false pride, superiority, and ego." He continued, "The other is good—he is joy, peace, love, hope, serenity, humility, kindness, benevolence, empathy, generosity, truth, compassion, and faith. The same fight is going on inside you—and inside every other person, too." The grandson thought about it for a minute and then asked his grandfather: "Which wolf will win?"

The old Cherokee simply replied, "The one you feed."

Some versions end there, but in the Cherokee world, the story and message continue.

"If you feed them right, they both win," the old Cherokee softly spoke. "You see, if I only choose to feed the white wolf, the black one will be hiding around every corner waiting for me to become distracted or weak and jump to get the attention he craves. He will always be angry and always fighting the white wolf. But if I acknowledge him, he is happy and the white wolf is happy and we all win. For the black wolf has many qualities—tenacity, courage, fearlessness, strong-willed and great strategic thinking—that I have need of at times and that the white wolf lacks. But the white wolf has compassion, caring, strength and the ability to recognize what is in the best interest of all.

"You see my grandson; the white wolf needs the black wolf at his side. To feed only one would starve the other and they will become uncontrollable. To feed and care for both means they will serve you well and do nothing that is not a part of something greater, something good, something of life. Feed them both and there will be no more internal struggle for your attention. And when there is no enemy within, you can listen to the voices of deeper knowing that will guide you in choosing what is right in every circumstance. Peace, my son, is the Cherokee mission in life. A man or a woman who has peace inside has everything. A man or a woman who is pulled apart by the war inside him or her has nothing."

Something changed in me that day the RV got stuck and I ended up immersed in the energy of "The Trail of Tears." Reflecting on that time over the past months, it occurred to me that lessons of the past are always presented again at some point in the future. The hardest lessons can teach us the most, if we are willing to listen to the voices that have come before us.

While the "Trail of Tears" officially ended in 1850, the residue and deep wounds on the ancestors of those souls that were marched thousands of miles while being treated as inhumanely as possible, continues to this day as the generations of Native Americans that followed attempt to restore their proud heritage.

Fifteen

Outer Limits

"With self-discipline most anything is possible."
—Theodore Roosevelt

In the "beginning," I really had no idea what it would take.

What I did know is I desperately wanted to be a better father to my children than my father was to me. But in many ways I had no concept of what was required to go past the limits that were already deeply imbedded in me since I was a small boy. Like so many men, I had no other blueprint than the one I was exposed to growing up and the "dad download" that takes place on a deep subconscious level, without our knowledge or permission. When I look at the early photos of myself, I see a boy full of potential, and a boy in pain. Those two opposites also can work together as we begin the process of overcoming what was, and creating what can be, as a father.

In order to do that, you must be willing to "boldly go where the men before you haven't gone" and that takes a concentrated effort, a fair amount of work (*on yourself*) *and* a serious dose of honesty to see what is true for you and what is not. Last but not least is the ability to understand your "unfinished business," as it were, the likes of which, if not taken care of by you, will become a burden and yoke your children will not only inherit but most likely repeat in their own lives. And when they become parents they too will get your "dad download" on that same subconscious level and will spend much of their own lives "undoing that which has been done."

Consider yourself the first and last line of defense, offense and any other metaphor you choose. "The buck stops here!" translates to "It begins and ends with me," for better or worse.

The first step in going past your self-imposed limits is admitting they exist. Beliefs are the rudder that guide our journey, hidden deep below the surface but there nonetheless. "Mind over matter" takes on a whole new meaning when it comes to being a 21ˢᵗ Century Dad, giving time and effort to those things that might have been overlooked by the fathers that have come before us. You have to decide what matters and what doesn't. You have to train your mind to go past what you think is possible for you.

Just like I did when I started the process of Dads Honor Ride.

In the first 53 years of my life, I can count on one hand with four fingers left over, the number of century rides (100 miles in one day) I did on a bicycle. And that was six years earlier when I was 48. I'm not exactly sure what prompted me to think, let alone start telling people, I planned to ride 100+ miles a day for three weeks without taking any days off. But, that's what I did for the three months leading up to the ride.

I have to make a confession. I've developed a passion for getting outside my comfort zone. What I've realized time and again is the real learning takes place when you expose yourself and make yourself vulnerable.

To emphasize the point, while on vacation in New Zealand, when our kids were ages 11 to 17, the seven of us went tandem skydiving with Skydive Wanaka. We also went bungee jumping off the Kawarau Bridge, which I found more challenging than jumping out of an airplane at 12,000 feet. Who would have guessed I would accompany my daughter Emily skydiving for her 18ᵗʰ birthday and go skydiving a year later with the U.S. Army Golden Knights?

I'm not sure where I found the time during the two months leading up to the ride, but I did eight rides of 100 miles or more, including three sets of two where I would ride 100+ miles two days in a row to get my butt acclimated to the anticipated discomfort of sitting on a small saddle. The first of those long training rides was a 200-kilometer (125-mile) ride in mid-April with a group of endurance riders known as the Great Lakes Randonneurs. Lon Haldeman, who I had met the week before, invited me to join him and his daughter Rebecca. He simply said "If you're serious about riding Route 66, you need to do as many century rides as possible. It's a ride, not a race and at a moderate pace it should take us about nine hours."

It must be mentioned that Lon is nothing short of a legend in the world of two-wheel racing and as a matter of fact, he was the catalyst for ultra-distance bicycle racing. His first achievement was in 1979 when he won the Wisconsin End to End Record covering 407 miles in 23 hours 7 minutes. In the 1982 Great American Bike Race, later renamed the Race Across America, he completely changed the parameters, cycling for 9 days and 20 hours with three other cycling pioneers. He's crossed the country over 85 times, including Route 66 more than two dozen times.

With all that in mind as the date for the 200-kilo ride approached, I remember thinking very deliberately, "If I don't accept his invitation, he'll know I wasn't serious and that might dim his interest in engaging in any future conversation." The counter thought I had was "What happens if I accept his invitation and I can't ride the entire 125 miles? That would be a total embarrassment." Thankfully, I decided to show up. We rode doing a large loop from Delavan, Wisconsin, and back getting our Randonneurs cards punched.

Just to clarify, Randonneuring is the term used to describe a type of long-distance cycling with its origins in audax cycling. In late 19th century Italy, day-long "challenge" sports became popular. Participants aimed to cover as much distance as possible and prove themselves *audax* meaning "audacious." In addition, a randonneuring event is called a randonnée or brevet, and a rider who has completed a 200-kilometer event is called a randonneur.

Did you get all that?

In randonneuring, riders attempt courses of 200 kilometers or more, passing through predetermined controls or check points, every few tens of kilometers. Riders aim to complete the course within specified time limits and receive equal recognition regardless of their finishing order. Riders may travel in groups or alone as they wish and are expected to be self-sufficient between controls.

The three of us rode at our own pace and as conditions allowed, shoulder-to-shoulder. The chance to spend nine hours riding with the legendary Lon Haldeman gave me just enough confidence to think, *if everything goes right over the next six weeks, maybe, just maybe, I can pull this off*. For the record, the last 15 miles were some of the hardest miles of any I would ride in preparation for the Dads Honor Ride.

The longest training ride I attempted was a ride to Milwaukee and back. A total roundtrip distance of 133 miles. I left at 8 a.m. with plans to meet Dr. Basil Salaymeh, one of my college buddies, for lunch. I arrived on time at the designated location. I called to let him know I was waiting, only to be informed by one of his assistants, his surgeries got pushed back and he regrets having to reschedule. I decided to have a quiet lunch and plan my return ride.

Shortly after I finished lunch, Bas called, apologized and said if it's not too late, he could be right over. When he arrived, he was stunned to learn I had ridden my bike from the Chicago area. I guess I had neglected to mention that when we made plans to meet. He had lunch, I had dessert, we caught up with one another and I was back on the road. It was a good ride and a good day, except for the fact it rained pretty heavily the last couple of hours and I wasn't quite outfitted for the wet conditions.

These two long training rides helped stretch me both physically and mentally. It got me thinking about being a dad. When the first child arrives, it's a total game changer. You start out blissfully ignorant about what it takes to be a parent and for the most part, it's baptism by fire. As the weeks and months roll by, you make the necessary shifts and adjust your priorities. God willing, when the second child arrives you go from 2-on-1 to man-to-man defense. It's a stretch, but again you make the necessary adjustments and change your priorities. If you're fortunate like we have been to have a third, fourth and fifth child you get used to stretching your limits and playing zone defense.

So in a way having five children has taught me invaluable lessons about taking on more and more responsibility in my personal life, in my business life and with the work I do in the community. Getting outside your comfort zone, as all leaders have come to understand, is where the real learning takes place. We're not talking about earning a college or graduate level degree but the more basic learning that allows you to reach deep and identify your own capacity.

The question, of course, then becomes, what are you capable of? What limits do you have to stretch? What beliefs do you have to let go of? What goals do you need to set? What course corrections need to be made in order to map out your journey to ensure the best possible outcome as it relates to being a father?

I didn't "know" I could complete that 125-mile ride until I got on the bike. Same goes for every time one of my kids got sick or a family situation came up that was a new experience. Sometimes you "fake it till you make it." Other times you simply do the best you can with what you have in the moment. Every single step as a father is, in some way shape or form, about taking you past your limits, what you thought you were capable of and often finding the crack of light in dark situations. Sometimes it's simply being a voice of reason and common sense when all about you seems to be out of control.

For eons, no one in the world thought it was possible for a human being to run a 4:00 minute mile on the track. In the 1952 Olympics in Helsinki, Brit Roger Bannister finished fourth which strengthened his will to go past the limits that had kept the 4:00 minute mark intact, a seemingly insurmountable barrier to break through. However, just two years later (and with minimal training as he was studying to become a doctor at the same time), Roger Bannister took to the track at Iffley Road in Oxford on May 6, 1954. When he reached the finish line, the announcer barely got the words out "The time was three . . ." before the crowd drowned him out, roaring their approval.

Bannister finished with a time of 3 minutes 59.4 seconds and a limiting belief was shattered along with a world record. It was as if Bannister gave permission to middle distance runners everywhere, when the record he set was broken just 46 days later.

In the 61 years since the day Bannister pushed back the limit of human achievement, it is no longer considered a wall. In 1964, Jim Ryun broke the 4-minute mile as a high school student. One year later, he broke his own record, with a time of 3:55.3 which then stood as the high school record for nearly 36 years. Steve Scott, from Upland, California, considered one of the best runners in American history, has run sub-4-minute miles 136 times in his career, more than any other runner in history.

And I thought biking was a workout.

So what changed? The mile didn't get any shorter and the clock didn't get any slower. All that was needed was an example of what is possible, and the barrier fell as if it had never existed.

So while you might never be next to me on a century ride, or set off to break the four-minute mile, you can look no further than the limits that have become part of your inventory as a dad. Once you get a little leverage on yourself, perhaps testing each one of those limits, to see if they move you forward or hold you back, would be a great place to start. *Remember*, it begins and ends with you.

Sixteen
Overcoming Obstacles

*"The supreme test of any civilization is whether or not
it can teach men to be good fathers."*

—Margaret Mead

One of my favorite phrases is "What doesn't kill you makes you stronger." With 100% certainty, you could say to each of my five kids "What doesn't kill you . . ." And they would respond ". . . makes you stronger." That mantra reminds me of the best-selling book *The Road Less Traveled* by the late M. Scott Peck, which begins with this truth—"Life is difficult." Dr. Peck's assertion is that until you accept the fact life is hard and far different than how it plays out in television sitcoms that resolve every problem in twenty-two minutes (without commercials) you will always struggle thinking it should be different than it is. You need to develop some grit and be accustomed to overcoming obstacles.

Rule number one, don't be afraid to fail. There is a 100% chance you won't succeed, if you don't try. Most anyone who has experienced any serious level of success has a laundry list of things they did poorly or couldn't do at all. We have all heard the Michael Jordan quote (and if you haven't here it is): "I've missed more than 9,000 shots in my career. I've lost more than 300 games, 26 times I've been trusted to take the game winning shot and missed. I've failed over and over again in my life. And that is why I succeed."

In a recent interview, Sylvester Stallone shared that he figured he "has failed 96% of the time" in his professional career as an actor and businessman. And then "Rocky" added, "it's the 4% that I have succeeded that has made the difference."

Every "overnight success" has spent years perfecting their craft and failing far more times than they succeeded. You don't get to success without first going through many failures, however, failure is not final. It contains the lessons that actually play a crucial role in the eventual outcome, the goal accomplished, the life well lived on "the road less traveled," as it were.

When looking back on the months of preparation for the DHR I see more clearly now how I was able to connect the dots. Physically disciplining myself to put in 1,800 miles of training in April and May was challenging from both a time commitment and the sheer physical challenge of riding for hours and hours, indoors as well as outdoors and in the rain. I was fortunate to build up my weekly mileage, stay healthy and injury free.

On the ride itself there were both physical and mental challenges. The physical obstacles include the steep climbs up the road to Prescott and then Flagstaff, each about 6,500 feet. On so many levels, my "attitude" helped me to overcome the "altitude" especially on the days there were headwinds and, thank God, I decided to ride from west to east so as to have more tailwinds and crosswinds. Some days the riding was both physically demanding and mentally defeating—something about not being able to see the enemy or know how long the headwinds will last.

Juggling a full-time job and sneaking in hour-long and, in some cases, day-long rides wasn't easy. What became increasingly challenging was the words of wisdom, no, actually words of caution I began to receive. Some would share horror stories of those who were catastrophically injured while bicycling, or worse yet, killed. Others, even those who had done some serious long-distance riding themselves, said it would be best to wait until the following year. Give yourself more time to train and plan the event. While I respected the advice and understood the logic, I rationalized, there would only be 12 more months of obstacles to overcome. Plus, when you have an idea and you have the passion to execute the idea, I always try to ask myself "If not now, then when?"

Being a dad is really no different. Parenting younger kids is physically demanding. It's normal to suffer sleep deprivation. There are feeding schedules to adhere to. You're changing diapers 24/7. You've got a ton of paraphernalia you're schlepping around including strollers, car seats, booster seats, and portable cribs, not to mention diaper bags, clothing and outerwear to be prepared for all occasions. Once the heavy lifting years start to lighten up, after three to five years in my experience, the challenge begins to shift from physical to psychological. By the time the kids get to middle school and high school they (and by definition you) are caught in the maelstrom of extreme social pressure being exerted on them and your family. Boys don't seem to be impacted as much as girls during these years, however, while they might not "show it," it is a factor. I found one of the best antidotes was to immerse myself in books on how to be a better dad and understand what's going on in their lives. Even more valuable was to talk with other dads with slightly older kids. Their insights and advice proved to be an invaluable resource.

Misleading sign said, "Road Closed."

In actuality it was "Bridge Out." Argh!

There is a concept that comes to mind that not only describes what it takes to ride with the wind (and against it) but also, at times, the fervent pitch and energy as a father that no one really tells you about, and often times you have to figure out as you go along. Its called "Specific Adaptation to Imposed Demands" or S.A.I.D for short.

It's a term used in kinesiology (the scientific study of the mechanics of human body movement), which tied right into my training for the Dads Honor Ride. Basically it means my body had to adapt to the demand I placed on it, over and over and over again, in order to perform at the highest level possible to endure and complete the journey. All the practice runs trained my "machine" to respond as it should. It would be near impossible to jump on a bike and ride like I did without prior training.

The toll on my body was a challenge, even with all my preparation. S.A.I.D is the reason bodybuilders look like they do, why swimmers look like they do. It's also why guys who sit on the couch and eat fast food but get no exercise look like they do. Your body is the depository for the demand (or lack of one) you place on it.

So what does kinesiology and the study of human movement have to do with being a 21st Century Dad?

That very same principle doesn't end with how we use our bodies, but also how we adapt to the demands of fatherhood, relationships and life in general.

As I mentioned earlier in the chapter, when my kids were small I was "learning the ropes" as it were, building up my muscles over a period of time based on my responses to the experiences I was having as a dad. As time went on, the demands changed but my ability to adapt was getting stronger. I was becoming more flexible and smarter (most of the time) in the process.

There is no more demanding role than that of a parent, and since most of us have zero to no training prior to our lifelong commitment, the only way we can "grow" into the job is by constantly immersing ourselves into the hands-on training, knowing that we are being prepared for when its "game time" comes in many different forms.

It's very important to understand the S.A.I.D principle is a powerful concept and having a greater awareness of the role it plays in fatherhood is crucial as it comes with a warning of sorts.

If you do not adapt to the demands of fatherhood, you and your children will suffer the consequences of a less than vibrant, honest and loving connection, a lifetime relationship.

Many of us grew up in a time when dads never spoke the words "I love you," and a generation of children would dismiss that lack of verbal validation with, "but I knew he loved me," all the while knowing deep down: not only do humans need to feel loved, they need to hear it, especially from their father.

Communication for many dads is a serious obstacle to overcome, mostly because, as pointed out, they didn't hear it growing up. Secondly, without that pattern to emulate, they find it tough to go within and pull the words out they longed to hear at one time. It's totally possible that instead of finding the courage to utter three simple words, they would rather continue on the pattern that has created so many deep rivers to cross over a lifetime of parenting. These are just another in a long line of beliefs handed down generation after generation, just waiting for someone to come along and change the direction of the river.

Beliefs are nothing more than information (true or not) that runs downhill in families washing over everyone and, unless challenged, they create the ongoing misery and distance between fathers and their children. The time when "do as I say, not as I do" has come to an end and along with it the concept of treating your children the way you were treated, unless it was a loving, healthy relationship, then carry on. If not . . . *stop it.*

You need look no further than Charles Darwin who explained it this way. "It is not the strongest of the species that survive, nor the most intelligent, but the one most responsive to change." His "theory of evolution," applies not only to iguanas but also to you as a father. Think about it. It's not your smarts or your strength (while both are important) that is the determining factor in your quest to become a 21st Century Dad . . . it's your ability to adapt to change.

Can you "Gumby Up" and be more flexible while retaining your formidable role as father? Can you see obstacles on the horizon your children are blind to and allow them the chance to grow through their mistakes without correcting their every move? Can you break the chains of the past and therefore seriously reduce the amount of wasted time and energy on being right instead of happy? Can you find time to connect with resources that are literally at your fingertips to become a better father, which might mean attending a conference or reading a book (you know, like this one)?

As a father, you are the common denominator in your child's life until the day you die, and for many years after. Your influence on them will be much like compound interest and, depending on what you invest in, the dividends will be either a loss or profit.

Final note here.

There is a marked difference between a "belief" which is defined simply as "a mental representation of an attitude positively oriented towards the likelihood of something being true" and a "knowing" which looks like this "awareness or understanding of someone or something which is acquired through experience or education by perceiving, discovering or learning."

It's not enough to have the "likelihood" that you are 21st Century Dad, or "believe" it might be true, but rather a concrete "knowing" that you are putting in the time developing The Quadrant (physically, mentally, spiritually and financially) that will help you overcome obstacles both past and present.

And if you love your kids, *tell them*. They shouldn't have to guess, wonder or even "believe" it. They should hear it and know it.

Seventeen
Enjoy the Ride

"Life is 10% what happens to us and 90% how we react to it."
—Charles R. Swindoll

Fatherhood is a serious issue to me, it has been my passion and purpose for nearly two decades, and a platform I am so very committed to. Many times over in this book, I have pointed out the dire consequences that are a result of father absence, even if the father is still in the home but pays little or no attention to his children. I have made every attempt to use the Dads Honor Ride experiences to bring forth hidden messages that underscore the importance of those four cornerstones (physically, mentally, spiritually and financially) that create a healthy, long-term relationship with our kids; and also the vast need for mentors: fathers that have gotten their act together and can teach their tricks of the trade to the next generation of dads, the latest model on the assembly line.

Along with all of that, comes this. *You have to enjoy the ride.*

No matter how many potholes you hit, speedbumps that might slow you down and flat tires you encounter along a lifetime, your job is to become a role model that is more important than any sports hero, pop star or actor. While my training was serious I had to remember that, in my case, taking a day off, a week off let alone three weeks off from work and family, to do something like a "Dads Honor Ride," I had to make sure to have the presence of mind to enjoy the ride. All work and no play is simply not healthy. This is not to suggest every mile of every day is fun and games. There were aspects of the ride itself that were very rewarding, like the feeling you get after a good workout.

Beyond the actual riding, we each need to seek out opportunities, to connect with people, places, local experiences, and just the sheer beauty of the local surroundings. The Western United States is an incredible spectacle and I took hundreds of pictures and videos to capture the moments and create permanent records of the experience.

First of all, what made the ride most enjoyable were the people, including the riders, the crew, and the extraordinary range of those we encountered along the way. One of the more interesting random encounters occurred in a hot tub one evening. There were three 20-something young guys and a woman about my age. They and their crew were literally caravanning from Boston the San Diego to participate in the upcoming annual R.A.A.M. (Race Across America) bicycle race. I was fascinated to learn about their four-man relay team strategy, which briefly involved two riders taking six hour shifts on and off. Each rider would ride as hard as they could for 30 minutes and then their partner would ride as hard as possible for 30 minutes. In the course of six hours, they would each ride three hours before taking a six-hour break. They expected to maintain an 18 mph pace and at that rate finish the entire distance in about eight days. If you do the math, that is about *400 miles a day*. That's to emphasize the difference between a *ride* and a *race*.

Meals always presented opportunities to bond with the other riders and crew as well as connect with those we happened to cross paths with. I pretty much had breakfast and dinner every day with Wilk and Lincoln Baker my Ride Director and owner of LIVE IT Adventures, an outdoor adventure company. As interested as people were in the Dads Honor Ride, the cause and the riders, it seemed more often than not they were just as interested in meeting and getting their photo with Wilk, the 89-year-old Tuskegee Airman. It was personally very satisfying to witness the warmth Wilk received from town to town. In some cases, it's the only time in their life they had ever met a WWII veteran of his ilk. Guys like me riding their bikes across the country? We're a dime a dozen.

One of the more memorable meals was at the Big Texan Steak House in Amarillo, Texas. We had been seeing billboard advertisements, for at least 100 miles, promoting their FREE 72-OZ. STEAK. You know the type of deal. It's "free" if you can down the whole thing in 60 minutes along with a baked potato, salad and for some unknown reason, three fried shrimp. By the time we got to the restaurant I was famished and was pretty certain the 72-oz. steak meal was part of my destiny. When else in my life would I be burning on average 8–10,000 calories a day? I watched two young guys who were taking the challenge, sitting underneath the countdown clock located above their table. They were both struggling and it was obvious they were not going to finish and would be paying the price (and for their meals). After about 20 minutes, I finally got some wisdom or maybe it was just plain common sense. I was convinced I could probably finish the massive 72-oz. steak, but then I started thinking, what would I feel like the next day? Would I have some gastronomical problems to add to the next day's road adventure? I opted for the 36-oz. version and added in some carrot cake just because.

It's often the little things in life . . . *like carrot cake* . . . that make moments matter more than they usually do.

I can tell you looking back over my life as a dad, with five children who all showed up with their own personality and presence, that the "good" always helped me through the "bad." While it might at times be a challenge to uncover the positive in a situation, at the end of the day you must find those "carrot cake moments" that make the journey all that much more enjoyable.

At the iconic Cadillac Ranch outside of Amarillo, Texas, with young Dave.

It was at times the simplest of things, like riding in the rain, (something a kid would do without hesitation) that brought me a sense of joy, the smell of water in the air and the hard ground absorbing the offering from the heavens. Having my son Dave along for the ride in the blistering heat and catching a glimpse of him pushing along the highway, reminded me of a time not that long ago when I taught him how to pedal without training wheels. My youngest daughter Addie next to me at the Rebel BBQ "Smoking Good-R-Way" in Blythe, California after riding 280 miles the first two days of the ride. It seems like just yesterday, she learned to use a fork without launching her food across the floor. Or the next day when we stopped for lunch in the middle of the desert at the Salome Cafe & Bar, located 54 miles west of Wickenburg, Arizona. The sign outside said "Bikers Welcome." I'm not sure I was the kind of "biker" they had in mind, but we were happy to get out of the hot sun and dust spirals. Lunch was punctuated by a lot of laughs and more dramatically, Lincoln doing the Heimlich Maneuver on Addie.

Day three of the journey was a long, hot steady 80-mile climb along U.S. 60 to Wickenburg, Arizona. While in Wickenburg we took delivery of the used 28' Majestic RV delivered by our friends from Cruise America which added a whole new dimension to the trip.

It became our *home away from home* . . . and it helped us to "enjoy the ride" literally speaking . . . with a renewed sense of purpose and spirit.

The average life expectancy for men is 77.6 years of age and 81.2 for women. That equates to 28,324 days that I may get to be alive. I was 28 when young Dave, our first child was born. So, I have been a dad for the past 26.5 years, or 9,672 days and counting. When it is all said and done, I will have been a father longer than any other role in my life except being a husband or son. A couple chapters back I pointed out the importance of being able to adapt to change, and part of the adaptability is enjoying the process, even though many times I didn't really understand the process at all.

The best part of all this? You can actually create "joy" by being mindful of your timeline, which might sound morbid, but it's also a great motivator when you fully understand that while you will always be a father, your children will grow up and become parents themselves. Soak up the moments, so when those inevitable days arrive when: they no longer need to be tucked in, the Tooth Fairy retires, their shoes no longer need tying, and homework no longer needs to be checked, you will have been conscious enough of the true value and meaning of being a dad. Soon enough there are more empty chairs at the dinner table and hugs get replaced by text messages. These moments and millions more like them are all part of the fatherhood experience, and are the very things that make the ride worth the effort.

As Ralph Waldo Emerson said, "Life is about the journey, not the destination." Enjoy the ride!!

Eighteen
Being Present

Faith is trusting God when life is out of control.

—Joel Osteen

I spent the first six weeks from the beginning of February to the middle of March, 2015, evaluating the probability of riding 2,300 miles in 21 days. Would that really be possible while at the same time holding down a full-time job and not abandoning my family responsibilities? Easy? NO! But keeping life in balance was my priority so there were many late nights *and* very early mornings to keep all the oars in the water. It wasn't until mid-March when I realized I needed to start putting in some more mileage. Initially because of the weather in the Midwest, I was riding a stationary bike indoors. As the temperatures and riding conditions improved, I was able to start riding outdoors.

While training, one of the techniques I had to learn is "keeping your mind off what your body is telling you." I had to find ways to "bypass the system" as it were, because my body had to be forced to go beyond its limits and the signals in my brain were often challenging to ignore. One of the easiest ways to do that for me is by listening to music.

Years ago the Sony Walkman was all the rage. (C'mon, you remember wearing that clunky musical robot on an armband or hooked to your belt with those unyielding earphones constantly getting in the way). Then the iPod came along and was revolutionary in so many ways, especially for those who exercise. Instead of playing cassette tapes with your Walkman, now you had more than a thousand songs at your fingertips in a sleek, hip, electronic device that was no bigger than a cassette tape. More recently the iPhone, which all but cannibalized the iPod, provided everyone, everywhere, with access to more than 100,000 apps. Pandora is one of the most popular music apps. Map My Ride is big in the running and riding community for keeping track of your mileage and workouts. What would we do without a Bluetooth to make and receive calls hands-free?

Pandora makes it super easy to set up various playlists for different types of music for different occasions. While training, I got in the habit of listening to Pandora for hours and hours giving a thumbs up to songs I'd like to hear again and a thumbs down to those I didn't.

I morphed from listening exclusively to Pandora to splitting my time listening to Joel Osteen on channel 128 on Sirius XM. At first, I thought what a cornball. Who is this guy with his southern twang and goofy jokes. What I have come to learn, over time, is he's a gifted communicator; he's funny, he's sincere, he's a devoted husband and a loving father. Plus, he's always talking about the influence his 'Daddy' had on him while he was alive and since he passed away 'to be with the Lord in 1999.' His homilies are always upbeat and full of inspirational stories about congregation members and family. Truth be told, I can listen to him hour after hour. I know virtually every punch line to every one of his jokes. In fact my favorite Joel Osteen sermon is #659, entitled "Blessings," which speaks to the role of fathers.

Given a choice to listen to the news or Joel, I'll choose Joel 100% of the time. There is really no benefit to bombarding your mind with the latest scandals or crimes all over the world. What I've found that works best for me is to start a workout or long ride listening to Joel and Victoria (his wife) and then a few hours later switch over to Pandora. I did this all throughout my training, which carried over to the Dads Honor Ride and pretty much every day since then.

I was fueling my body with the high calorie, high protein drinks I found most palatable and I was nurturing my mind with upbeat spiritual messages. I did this right up until June 15, which was the beginning of week three of DHR. We had already travelled over 1,500 miles. I had been proclaiming for weeks my intent to call into *The Joel Osteen Show*, which broadcasts live every Monday at 6 p.m. central time, to see if they would take my call. As fate would have it, I was the first caller that Monday. It was a thrill to talk with Joel and Victoria. I remember Joel sounding in disbelief about an old dad like myself, riding his bike 2,300+ miles. Victoria made a reference to the scripture verse from Proverbs 27:17 about "as iron sharpens iron, so one person sharpens another." Referring to me, by example, helping sharpen other fathers.

The actual call lasted no more than five minutes, but it was a transformative experience. After hanging up and reflecting on the conversation and the first two weeks of the ride, I had one of those light bulb moments. It all of a sudden dawned on me. A week from now, I'm going to be sitting at my desk and doing the same job I had been doing for 30 years. While I love my job, our clients and the people I work with, there is only so much satisfaction you can get from doing the same thing, day in and day out, for three decades.

In my mind I jumped the chasm from trying to pass the time and making it go more quickly to wanting to slow time down and more fully enjoy the last week of the ride. It was at that point I made the decision to turn off Pandora and turn off Joel Osteen. At first the quiet didn't feel right, but I wanted to be more present to see and experience where I was, and not just get to the end destination every day.

It was, without question, a spiritual mind shift. I realized what worked for me in training and the first two weeks of the ride was effective to keep my mind off my body, but it had the unintended consequence of limiting the depth of my experience.

It took two weeks and more than 1,500 miles to realize "I think I've got this." I think I can do this whole ride, providing I can stay healthy and be safe. I can immerse myself in this "vision quest" on two wheels, absorb and extract the sights and sounds that are part of a "once in a lifetime experience."

I offer my deepest thanks to Joel and Victoria for helping me come to this realization. It served me well for the last week of the ride and then when I returned to my daily routine. As a result of that experience, I find myself seeking ways to be more present, more in the moment, every day. It's where life is actually taking place. Not in the past or in the future, but right here and now.

We live in amazing times, even though it often appears technology is surpassing our humanity. The ability we have to connect to one another, gather every bit of information on every subject known to humankind, store thousands of songs in a little machine and get hundreds of channels on the giant flat screen is far beyond what any other group of humans who inhabited the earth before us ever experienced.

As a matter of fact, Americans have made their television a part of the family. According to Nielsen, in 2015, the average home in the U.S. has 2.54 people living in it, but has 3.0 television sets. The average time spent saying "there's nothing to watch" each day is about five hours and interestingly enough, 49% of people surveyed say they watch too much television. As a side note, the average 12-year-old spends 900 hours in school per year, and watches television about 1200 hours over the same time period. Electronic babysitter indeed.

As a father, making sure your kids don't get totally hooked into the electronic landfill of television is one thing but, as adults, we don't fare much better. The average adult (over 18) will spend *nine years of their life* watching television. For men, a majority of that time is sports and news. That kind of learned behavior can lead to one of the biggest forms of father absence.

DDS or "Distracted Dad Syndrome."

While it's important to have an outlet after putting in some serious time at work, nothing can be more debilitating to a healthy family dynamic, than having valuable time together wasted by everyone looking away from each other watching excessive hours of programming, especially when you consider that most of the content contains so much violence. By the time a kid turns 18 years old they will have, on average, witnessed 150,000 acts of violence masked as "entertainment" combined with being bombarded by thousands and thousands of commercials that basically tell them they need a certain product to become an improved version of themselves. This combination of messages about the world *and* who they are in relation to the images they see is even more reason to be as fully present with them as you possibly can.

Forgoing conversation or connection with your children because "the game" is on or having so many televisions in the home that after dinner (if dinner actually happens with everyone at the table) each family member goes off into their own "space" to watch their shows, is a clear example of father absence, even while you are physically home. "Pay per view" takes on a whole new meaning when you consider the hefty price we pay for spending time watching "reality" shows, while our own "reality" slips by . . . unnoticed.

The same goes for smartphones and the aforementioned iPod/iPhone. Take a walk in downtown Chicago and a majority of people are hooked up to the devices that have now become our electronic parasitic twin. They are connected to the machine but not to the world around them, often carrying on a conversation out loud about their latest drama, scam or love life. Distracted driving has gotten so bad, April is now "Distracted Driving Month" designated to remind teenagers (and adults) that 3,200 people die each year because they were texting or talking on the phone while attempting to operate three tons of metal at 50 mph.

We are more "connected" than ever before, but to what?

When it comes to fulfilling the role of being a 21ˢᵗ Century Dad, a quote from the late, great cartoonist Bil Keane (creator of "Family Circus" that according to King Features Syndicate is the most widely syndicated cartoon in the world since it debuted in 1960, appearing in 1,500 newspapers) who said, "Yesterday's the past, tomorrow's the future, but today is a gift. That's why it's called the present."

How we invest or spend our time is a personal decision. Being "present" with and for your children is the greatest "gift" you will ever give them.

Nineteen
Drafting

"If you want to go fast, go alone. If you want to far, go together."
—African Proverb

Being very mindful of the complexities of the English language, I wanted to make sure when you got to this chapter titled "Drafting" you understood right off the bat it was not about a high school class on technical drawing, or when an athlete gets plucked from the college ranks to the pro's or compulsory military service. Matter of fact, it has more to do with Canadian Geese than humans, but more about that in a moment.

If you're in a competitive bicycling event like an Ironman triathlon, it's illegal to draft or "slipstream" behind another rider, using the lead rider as windshield of sorts to pull you along just a little bit faster. It's kind of like when you are on the highway and get behind a semi-truck that is tooling along and if you get close enough behind the rig, you actually get pulled along in the vortex of the wake of wind it creates.

There were a host of benefits to having other riders participate in the Dads Honor Ride for a day or multiple days. I enjoyed the camaraderie, sharing stories and experiences, meeting new people, making friends and strengthening existing relationships all come to mind. While it didn't happen often, it was beneficial to be tucked in, wheel to wheel, behind someone else. While the view doesn't change when you're staring at someone's butt, you do develop a certain appreciation when someone is shielding the wind and running interference like blockers in football. It allows you to lower your output and preserve your strength, even if only for a few miles here and there and when you're in the saddle for 7 to 10 hours a day, you have some time to think about a lot of things and the benefit to drill a down a little deeper.

On one of those deeper dives, I got to thinking about other men and fathers who have played an important role in my life. The men I could "draft" off of when it came to many twists and turns, ups and downs of being a dad—men I could trust and "get behind" to understand their experiences to help pull me along the path.

More recently, I am very thankful for the role some good friends and new acquaintances played in an effort to prepare me for the 21-day, 112-miles per day Dads Honor Ride. Starting with my good friend Bob Lee who is one of the most respected long-distance *solo* riders in our little town of Barrington, Illinois. Bob has completed three charity rides known as "A Ride For Three Reasons," raising awareness and funds for Cancer, Hospice and ALS (Lou Gehrig's Disease). For the record, "solo" means you're self-supported, which means no RV or chase vehicles, no one doing bike repairs or helping you navigate the route and, in many, cases camping out. Bob's first ride in 2001 was 3,200 miles from San Diego to St. Augustine, Florida. He celebrated his 65th birthday by riding 6,500 miles on his second ride in 2007 from Jacksonville, Florida, to Sea Harbor, Maine and across to Anacortes, Washington (as in the state of Washington). Bob's third ride in 2012 was from Vancouver, British Columbia to Tijuana, Mexico a distance of 2,500 miles. If you do the math it adds up to over 12,000 miles that Bob has pedaled to raise funds and awareness. As a cancer survivor himself, he understands the great need for research funding. If the distance alone wasn't impressive enough, I think it's also important to mention Bob is now 74 years old and still going strong.

When the idea to do a cross-country bicycle ride first entered my mind, Bob was the first person I needed to talk with, even before bringing it up with Peggy. Over a soda one Sunday afternoon in early February, Bob explained how he planned and executed his rides. I told him I was contemplating the 2,300-mile ride from Santa Monica to Chicago sandwiched in the three weeks between Addie's high school graduation on May 30 and Father's Day, June 21. His first response was to offer some words of caution. He said the rule of thumb for endurance riders is to take one day off a week. It would be too risky to ride 21 days in a row without wiggle room for severe weather conditions, let alone fatigue, minor injuries or equipment issues. The big take away from that first conversation was I was definitely not interested in being a solo rider. I didn't have the experience or the desire to be a DIY (do it yourself) rider.

Meeting with Bob also provided me with a little cover for what was sure to be a touchy conversation when I broached the idea for the ride with Peggy. I started that conversation by saying "I was talking with Bob Lee about doing a long-distance bike ride to raise funds for fatherhood charities. He provided me with some invaluable insights." After getting past the When, What, Where, Why, and How, I explained the need to do a lot more research before committing to such a task. I remember Peggy saying "If that's how you want to spend those three weeks, that's on you. Don't count on me to be driving any RV and I'm definitely not interested in riding." My antennas were alert for the word *no*. Not hearing *No*, by default in most men's minds means . . . *Yes* . . . mine included.

I spent the next few weeks trying to evaluate the logistics and probability of success. At my annual physical in early February, I mentioned to my internist Dr. Greg Ewert, I was contemplating riding Route 66 during the three weeks leading up to Father's Day. I recall him saying, "You're one of my healthier 50-something-year-old patients and one of the very few not on some prescription medication(s)." He said, "If you can put the time in to train I would be more concerned about getting hit by a vehicle and getting injured or killed."

He also mentioned he had another patient, Dr. Jason Conviser, who helped a severely injured guy do a cross-country trip. That introduction to Jason put me on an entirely different trajectory.

Jason, who is an exercise physiologist, had spent four years from 2008 to 2012 helping a 52-year-old guy recover from some catastrophic injuries and prepare for a long-distance ride. Jason agreed to meet for a Saturday morning breakfast in Evanston, where he lives. He also brought along Lincoln Baker, another fellow from Evanston, who was involved with helping the injured guy do his bike ride. As I learned at breakfast, Lincoln was the ride director for the 78-day ride from San Diego to St. Augustine, Florida (for you ride junkies, it was a 3,129-mile ride). Jason, who is my age, was lukewarm at best on the idea for a 21-day, 2,300+ mile ride.

Lincoln, who is considerably younger, was more of the attitude: *nothing ventured nothing gained.* Being a glass half full type of person, I gravitated to Lincoln's reaction to my ride. That meeting and the subsequent relationship Lincoln and I developed would snap a big piece of the puzzle in place. Lincoln would sign on to be the Dads Honor Ride ride director. He had his own 23-foot trailer already outfitted as a mobile bike station. He's an expert at all things related to bikes, like a real life MacGyver. He's also an EMT, so God forbid, if something happens, I've got someone to be a first responder. He was just the right person at just the right time. Plus his wife, Courtney Riley, an Ironman triathlete, as it turned out would ride the first few days of the ride.

It gets even better . . . here's the more amazing part of the story. The injured guy that Jason and Lincoln helped do that 3,129-mile ride is Mark Stephan, a retired Goldman Sachs partner. The short story is, on August 11, 2007, Mark was riding his bicycle with a small group of friends on the North Shore in Chicago. He had an accident where he was thrown over the front of his handlebars fracturing his C2 and C3 vertebrae. He was diagnosed with central cord syndrome, a broken neck and pinched spinal cord. He spent a month in intensive care at Northwestern Hospital without any feeling or sensation from the neck down. He was told he would never walk again or have any use of his limbs.

Four and a half years later with extraordinary therapy from the Rehabilitation Institute of Chicago (RIC) and help from doctors like Jason, Mark was preparing to do the unthinkable, ride a customized recumbent tricycle from coast to coast. It would take Mark 78 days to cover the 3,129 miles, but he finished the ride in July of 2012.

But wait . . . *It gets better.* Unrelated to the conversations with Jason and Lincoln I was talking with another friend Gerry Keenan about helping out with logistics. Gerry is a consultant, a former partner at Price Waterhouse (one of my alma maters), a Deacon at Sacred Heart Parish and president of Zanmi Sasye-Partners with Sassier, Inc. a nonprofit serving residents in rural Haiti. In an email, on Saturday, February 20 (the same day I first met with Jason and Lincoln), Gerry mentioned that Mark Stephan was going to be speaking at the annual meeting of his Sacred Heart's Men's Club the following Monday. Would I be interested in attending?

I used to think life is full of a bunch of coincidences, but now I'm pretty certain the Almighty has a hand in such things. So two days later I show up at the Indian Hill Club in Winnetka for the SHMC meeting to be followed by dinner. I arrived about 30 minutes early. There were just a handful of folks present and setting up the room. I introduced myself to one of the volunteers and indicated I was a guest of Deacon Keenan. I mentioned how excited I was to hear Mark's story. The person said, "If that's the case, why don't you introduce yourself to Mark. He's sitting over there." We spoke briefly until the room started to fill up and everybody started coming up to Mark to say hello and thank him for coming to speak.

Let me paint a very vivid picture if I can. Mark is a person of modest stature. We're about the same age and we each spent most of our careers in the world of investments. He gets around on forearm crutches. It took him a couple of minutes to navigate across the room, a distance of about 60 feet.

Between that initial conversation, listening to his presentation and then sharing dinner with him afterwards, my head was spinning. At one level I was thinking if a guy who, by some definition, is a functional quadriplegic can ride his bike from coast to coast, an able-bodied person should be able to do the same. He said in a very matter of fact tone, "If Lincoln (the guy I had met just two days before) is available to be your ride director, he's your man."

Of all the things Mark and I talked about, the most profound takeaway was what he told me about how he was able to surpass the extraordinary obstacles he encountered from the time of his injury to completing his ride. He said "Instead of thinking I was doing therapy for four years, I adopted the attitude I was 'training.' Training is something I could relate to having previously done marathons and triathlons. Therapy is something other people have you do to recover from an injury. Training is something you do to prepare yourself to accomplish a goal or dream." He said quite simply "It's a mindset."

As a small token of my appreciation, I presented him with a Great Dads Coin and thanked him profusely for his time. We would go on to have a series of conversations over the next few months. Thank you, God.

It turned out Lincoln was available and, as instructed, I hired him to help me figure out how to get from point A to point B. Within the span of a few weeks from that initial conversation with Bob Lee, to my doctor's visit with Greg Ewert, to my breakfast with Jason and Lincoln, to my introduction to Mark Stephan through my friend Gerry Keenan, I was drafting in a way I could not have predicted or imagined. We still had to navigate an obstacle course of logistics the next 100 days, but it felt like I was operating on rocket fuel.

Oh yeah . . . those Canadian Geese.

No doubt you have seen flocks of geese flying in "formation." There is good reason for their flight plan. These incredible birds might be a bit of a nuisance on the ground, but up in the air they have some powerful lessons to teach us about "drafting" as it pertains to fatherhood. Studies have shown that the whole group of birds can fly 71% further by staying together than by going it solo. When one bird falls out of formation, it will immediately regain its slot to take advantage of the power generated by so many wings and actually be "lifted up" back to where it belongs. Over long distances, the lead bird will eventually get tired and slowly make its way to back of the line where it can be pulled along, rest and regain its strength. While it might not always be heard from the ground, Canadian Geese are always "honking" or communicating and encouraging one another, making sure all the birds know what is going on.

Finally, and perhaps most importantly, these birds will leave no goose behind. Should one become injured and grounded, two other geese will fly out of formation and stay with their feathered friend until it recovers . . . or dies.

Find your flock and get in their draft. Stay in formation and share the responsibilities whether you are the lead bird or the support honker in the back. Communicate, encourage and stick by your flock and make sure that no goose . . . or dad . . . is left behind.

Twenty

The 1% Solution

"Any man can be a father, but it takes someone special to be a dad."
—Proverb

If it hasn't yet become apparent to you, I'm a numbers guys. I can't explain how or when it happened but my brain somehow, someway got wired for numbers. For the record, I wasn't blessed with a photographic memory. Actually, quite the contrary: there are days I can't even remember what I had for lunch the day before. For me, numbers are "sticky" for lack of a better term, they seem to lodge themselves in my gray matter.

For most people they can recite their social security number, maybe their driver's license number and handful of friends and family members' phone numbers (but with speed dial even those numbers are getting harder to remember). For some reason my numbers brain goes a step further to credit card numbers and passwords. In most areas of life, it's not a particularly useful trait, but with the type of work I do as a financial advisor it comes in handy.

At one time or another we have all had a little experience back in school about a basic economic concept called the "Bell Curve," which is a way of depicting the probability of outcomes. Without doing brain surgery, let me add to that the concept known as "Standard Deviation" (stay with me on this, I promise there is a method to my madness on this stuff). It's generally understood that 68% of all outcomes are within one standard deviation from the middle, otherwise known as the *majority of outcomes* that make of the big part of the bell shape. If you were to calculate out to two standard deviations, you can account for *95% of all outcomes.* The other 5% are considered less statistically likely. In a normal distribution, 2.2% of the outcomes are much better than average including all the best outcomes. In the opposite direction, the other 2.2% of the outcomes are all the worst outcomes.

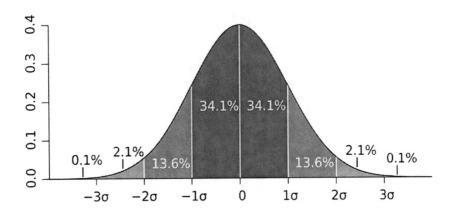

So what does this have to do with fathering or the Dads Honor Ride? Let's start with kids and the probability of them achieving their full potential. High school graduation rates are a basic telltale for determining the likelihood of being economically independent. Sadly 3,200 youth drop out of U.S. high schools every day. That's an estimated 1.68 million kids per year in the U.S. who will not earn a high school degree.

You might say so what? School isn't for everyone. Why should I care? Did you know that 71% of high school dropouts come from father-absent homes? Did you know that 75% of all crimes in America are committed by high school dropouts? And that 85% of incarcerated youth come from father-absent homes? Consider also that kids from father-absent homes are four times as likely to grow up in poverty and nine times more likely to drop out of high school. All of a sudden you realize that when someone else's kids drop out of high school, it's not just their problem, it becomes our problem and compound interest of the worst kind.

So who is to blame and what can be done? I'm not a blame-game type, but the low graduation rates are partially a result of our outdated and, at times, ineffective public school system. It is shocking that the U.S. ranks number 22 out of the 27 developed countries for the percentage of youth who graduate from high schools.

While the schools take a lot of flak for low graduation rates (and some of it is deserved) the *root problem* is too many kids are coming from single parent families. Like any assembly line, if you keep putting broken components in the system, why would you expect to get good products coming out?

Research shows that when both parents are involved in the educational lives of their children, high school graduations go up dramatically and a lot of the issues that take kids down, like drug and alcohol abuse, teen suicide and pregnancy, crime and incarceration all improve. Simply because there was a dad involved in the education of their child.

While the "problems" seem complicated, the truth is the "answers" are really quite simple. The "effects" of the problem are what show up on the never ending news cycle about young people taking each other's lives, the influence of gangs that take the place of a "family" and the constant threat of all the aforementioned things that threaten their existence. The "cause" or solution lies at home, and I am convinced it's called "Dad."

Another reason I think that 'life is a numbers game' has to do with the type of tenacity and persistence required to get ahead. Here's a real-life example to illustrate my point. When I first got into the brokerage industry 31 year ago, there were a variety of ways to pursue new business development, including: seminars, advertising, mailers and networking, but the time tested and expected way was to cold call. We were expected to make at least 100 calls a day. Do the math that's 500 calls per week, 2,000 calls per month and a whopping 24,000 cold calls per year.

Just making the calls was no guarantee for success, but you dramatically enhanced the probability of being able to be part of the 15% who still had a job after two years. Yes, that's right. Predictably, 85% of the people who started were gone within two years. Furthermore, for every 100 calls made, I could expect to get through about a third of the time. Of the 33 people I actually spoke with, two thirds of them would give me a quick no and sometimes with a little profanity or perhaps a reference to my mom or sister, which was always interesting. Of the remaining 10 or 11 who would listen, I would follow up with some information and my business card. One of those 10, over the course of 12 to 18 months might do business with me.

So let me recap. For every 100 calls made, I was doing well if I had a 1% success ratio. I literally built my entire career on that 1%. The reason most people don't' succeed is they can't deal with the 99% rejection. Those tens of thousands of phone calls taught me a great lesson . . . not to take things personally.

Even though I heard a fair amount of negativity when I shared the objective of riding 2,300+ miles in 21 days, I tried to discern who was giving me advice on how to overcome obstacles and who was just being negative because that's their personality. It's always important *to consider the source* when seeking feedback or advice.

So how can adopting the concept that you can succeed with a 1% success attitude improve your odds in becoming a better dad? You're going to try things at different stages of your child's development. The 1% solution is to be *persistent*. Kids, especially when they become teenagers, can be very difficult to communicate with. After all, what could you possibly know, you're the lame parent. If you're prepared for this attitude and understand it's more about their stage in life, you won't take it personally. The level of drama will be lower.

Much of what I learned hammering the phones in those early years of my career rolled over into the toolbox I carry as a father. The message then is this: *be persistent and **never give up**, no matter what the situation*. You're their dad. You're the one who is supposed to be present, not just in the easy times when the sun is shining, but also when the clouds roll in and life gets messy. Also, modeling the "I'm here for you no matter what" philosophy is something you want your kids to emulate when they mature.

The pace of life in the 21st century is a daunting task to keep up with, and sometimes you won't be able to make it to ALL of the games, plays, dinners, movies and more. However, keeping the 1% solution top of mind, you can find ways—*small as they might seem*—to be a big part of your kids' lives. That little extra effort, the call when they least expect it (*even if you have to leave a voicemail*) a text (*it's great way to let them know you are around, even if they don't answer*) a note in their lunch, or under their pillow or even in the car when they start driving, all add up over time. Keeping the lines of communication open, making those "cold calls" even if the relationship is strained from divorce or difficult because of distance, go a long way to using the Bell Curve in your favor and while it might take some time, the outcome will be worth that little bit of extra effort.

You might not be able to give 110 % all the time, but 1%, is not only doable but makes the absolute difference when it comes to success, whether you are building your business, your life or a strong, positive and lasting relationship with your children.

Twenty-One
Words Count

"I have fought the good fight, I have finished the race, I have kept the faith."
—2 Timothy 4:7

I have a deep connection to numbers, not only as a major part of my career but also the number of miles I rack up while riding. I am constantly pushing my boundaries and comfort zone with each role carrying a certain significance. So I was fascinated to find out that there are 1,025,109 words in the English language as concluded by the Global Language Monitor which also states the millionth word threshold was crossed on June 10, 2009 at 10:22 a.m. (GMT) with the addition of the controversial "Web 2.0" entry. Currently, there is a new word created every 98 minutes or about 14.7 words per day.

No wonder we often have a hard time understanding each other. When I was growing up, kids talked to each other. Now they sit in the same room and text each other.

Communication is the bedrock for developing and maintaining relationships, whether personal or professional. We communicate messages consciously and subconsciously all the time. In many instances the non-verbal messages we send are louder and more clear, than those we speak. It could be as simple as the way you hold yourself, the type of eye contact you make or don't make when speaking to someone, the firmness of your handshake, the way you wear your hair, and your attention to detail with your personal hygiene.

We are also bombarded by information through our senses of sight, smell and touch. One's sense of awareness filtered through their lifetime of experience provides a clearer understanding of how to read and interpret various situations. For the purposes of this chapter, I'd like to focus on the importance of verbal communication and maybe just a little more about the written word.

It's pretty well understood that your thoughts are your own, but once spoken they are no longer yours. In some instances, how you say something may deliver a different message than the one you intended. Have any of you married guys ever had your spouse say, "I don't like the way you said that," or some variation of that message?

The simple truth is men and women communicate differently, which was the focus of the classic best-seller from 1992 by author and relationship counselor John Gray, entitled *Men Are from Mars, Women Are from Venus*. It's a must read and, I would argue, re-read for those committed to having a more secure relationship.

As men we need to own that we're not wired as emotional creatures in the same way as women. That's not to say we can't get better at reaching that part of ourselves. I think we would be better communicators if we did more listening and opened up about our feelings. Let me be quick to say, I've become a better listener over the years, but I still struggle with expressing my feelings. It's just my nature.

While out on the ride, I was deeply touched by the many calls I received from family and friends just checking in to see how I was doing. For the most part I could just swipe my iPhone and accept the call, which went to the same Bluetooth device I used to listen Pandora and Joel Osteen. It was typically a little hard to hear (on both ends) due to the wind or road noise with cars and trucks whooshing by.

The periodic calls I received from Bob Lee and Lon Haldeman, two of my biking buddies from back home, were like little boosts of energy. There I was, in most cases, riding in the middle of nowhere and a friendly voice breaks through the monotony of the road with a friendly "just checking in on you to see how things are going."

I also remember receiving multiple calls from my good friend Lou Weisbach, one of my tennis buddies. It was great to be reminded that folks where thinking about and praying for me, taking time out of their day to connect into mine, wherever I might have been on the map.

One of the most meaning and memorable of those calls was from Clarke Garnett, one of my best friends from high school and a guy who was in our wedding party 32 years earlier.

It was day number eight, June 8. I had to get up a couple of hours earlier than normal to do an in-studio interview at the local NBC affiliate and I was supposed to be there at 6 a.m. Since they told me to bring my bike, I thought I'd ride the few miles there even though it was still pitch black. I arrived at the prescribed time and had a really good interview with the anchor Kim Tobin who asked the right questions and gave the space for some really good answers to underscore the mission of the Dads Honor Ride.

In studio at NBC4 in Albuquerque with Kim Tobin.

Immediately afterward, while still at the NBC studios, I did a phone interview with Lisa Dietlin and Andy Busch for a weekly podcast he hosts called *Engage with Andy Busch,* that would air on or around Father's Day. It was a fun experience and Andy and I agreed to meet after Father's Day, when I was back in Chicago. Then it was back to the hotel for a quick bite to eat and back on the road by 7:30 a.m.

I remember the route through downtown Albuquerque during rush hour as being a little dicey, the energy of the heavy rush-hour traffic as I made my way out of town starting to take a toll on me.

About two hours later and no more than 30 miles into the ride, my legs felt very heavy. I felt fatigued and a little disoriented. I couldn't quite figure out what the problem was. I had the same food, the same nutrition and hydration. As I recounted my usual routine I realized the only thing that was different was I gotten about two hours less sleep than most of the previous seven nights. That change in my inner clock (for someone who doesn't normally need more than four to five hours of sleep) was the difference in making this potentially a very long day.

I remember sitting under a tree outside some fast food restaurant and I texted the crew to let them know I was taking a break. I felt deflated like one of the flat tires I had gotten on the ride. Now I needed a patch, of sorts, and to be pumped back up to my own personal operational PSI (pounds per square inch) in order to reach Santa Rosa, New Mexico, that day's destination.

My phone rang and it was my old high school buddy Clarke Garnett (his actual name is Edward Clarke, but I call him EC), calling from Virginia where he and his significant other Leslie live. I had visited with the two of them two months earlier, while there on a business trip. While they are both super fit and considered doing a leg of the ride, they couldn't squeeze it into their busy schedules.

This is how that conversation went.

"Hello," I said.

"Hey buddy, it's Clarke, how are you doing?"

"EC, great to hear from you. I'm somewhere 30 miles east of Albuquerque having a pity party for myself and feeling more fatigued than at any time during the first seven days. What are you up to?"

He responded, "Oh, that's right. You're on your bike ride. I had forgotten about that with all that has transpired recently. I was calling to share some really sad news with you. Leslie's 20-year-old daughter, Madeline, committed suicide two weeks ago. As a close friend I thought you should know."

My heart slumped and there was an elongated pause. "Oh my God," I said. "I'm so sorry to hear that." We talked further about how hard it was for Leslie and her family to accept Madeline's decision to take her own life, after battling with severe depression for several years.

Sadly, Clarke was uniquely prepared to be there for Leslie. It was back in August of 2000, when Clarke's oldest son Brian, who was then 15, died suddenly in a car crash when the driver, another teenager, lost control of the vehicle and t-boned into a tree.

At the end of the call, I offered my sincere condolences to Leslie and her family. He wished me good luck on the rest of the ride and we hung up. I sat there a bit numb from the tragic news. Here they were grieving the loss of this beautiful 20-year-old young woman. What's my problem? I didn't get enough sleep? I'm feeling fatigued? It's as if whatever problems I was experiencing just melted away. The pity party I was having for myself ended and I was back on the road. That call, those words, had a very profound impact on me then and still do today. Another coincidence? I think not. For me, it confirmed The Holy Spirit was present. Message received.

This chapter is on the importance of communication and letting people know your thoughts and feelings. Speaking words that uplift and inspire are a critical part of being a great dad. The late John R. Powers who, according to a mutual friend, was a world class dad, and author of several books including the best-selling classic which became a musical play, *Do Black Patent Leather Shoes Really Reflect Up?* (His classic comic novel of the 1960s Catholic subculture stars a Chicago boy who learns about the important questions in life, while at an all-boys Catholic school on Chicago's South Side.). John wrote a letter to his second daughter, Joy Victoria, shortly after she arrived on the planet. I don't think more eloquent words have been written to express what every father should feel in their heart, and communicate to their children.

Dear Child of Mine,

As I look into your eyes for the very first time, I cannot begin to understand the emotions that are gushing within my soul. I don't know you at all. How could I? You're 20 minutes old, in an hour you will have already lived another three lifetimes. But already I love you differently, and more deeply, than I have ever loved anyone before. I would die for you. Birthdays are about presents, so on this very first birthday, let me give you gifts that will last as long as I live.

I give you the gift of freedom. Every moment of your infancy, every moment of your childhood and certainly every moment of your teenage years, you'll be moving away from me. That's the way it should be. At first the movements will be so small I won't even notice them, but one day I will look up and I'll see the distance between us . . . and I'll wonder why I never saw it before. And that distance will only continue to grow until that day arrives for the first time, when you truly walk out of my life. Come back because you want to, not because you have to.

I give you the gift of rejoicing in who you are . . . and not who I want you to be. I will remind myself that I am not raising a mirror, that you are not here to grasp what was beyond my reach, you're not here to complete my unfulfilled dreams. You're not here . . . to live my life again. You are here to celebrate your existence in the way you choose.

I give you the gift . . . of me . . . all of me. In my mind you will never be more than a thought away. My ears will hear your whispers and your sighs, your laughter, your cries, your triumphs and your tragedies. My eyes will try to see the world as you see it, young . . . exciting . . . loving. You will hear my voice even if I cannot speak, teaching you, encouraging you, guiding you, correcting you . . . how special you are. My shoulder is there for you to lean on, my arms will always long to hug you and carry you where you want to go. To hold you back when I know I must, to let you go when I know I should. My hands will pat you on the back, applaud your efforts and nudge in the direction we both know is true. Hopefully, my feet will leave footsteps you'll want to follow, but won't run after you, when you want to leave.

Every day you will give me the gift of being who you are, doing what you do, living your life the way you choose.

Like all gifts, mine are free . . . you don't owe me . . . anything.

But perhaps one day you'll take these gifts, re-wrap them in your own special way, and give them to the gleam, I now see in your eyes.

Dear Child of Mine, Happy Birthday.

What powerful words from a father to his child, what a lesson in communication.

Never underestimate the impact a call, a word of encouragement or acknowledgment or a letter might have on your son or daughter, some other young person or simply an acquaintance.

Keep in mind that before you say a word, you are its master; once you say a word, you are its servant.

The words you bring forth take on a life of their own, lodging themselves into a conversation that may seem to end but in reality never does. What we say today, for better or for worse, stays with us for a lifetime, like these words Dr. Powers's grandfather shared with him as a young man:

"You are truly never an adult, until you consider all of the children of the world . . . yours."

As a father, I totally understand what those words mean and part of the fuel keeps me going—be it on a 2,300+ mile bike ride, handing out Great Dad Coins or supporting the many friends and mentors that have crossed my path—it comes down to the most simple of all concepts: Words can either build bridges or create ditches.

While actions speak louder than words, words count. We need to choose them wisely.

Onwards and upwards!

At the end of the ride. A celebratory pose.

From left to right: last day riders: Bob Lee, Patrick Wierzchucki, Jorge Solorio, David & Peggy Hirsch and Darek Cupial

On field during pre-game at U.S. Cellular Field.
Left to right: Lawton "Wilk" Wilkerson, David Hirsch and Tom Dreesen

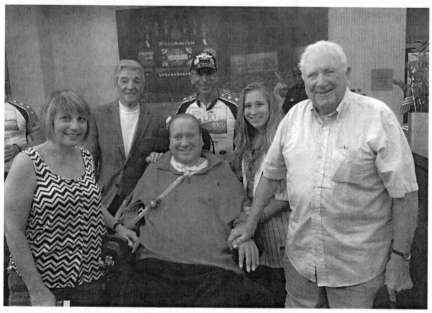

At U.S. Cellular Field after the game.
Front row, from left to right: the Mullen family—Athena, Jim, Maggie and John
Back row, from left to right: Tom Dreesen and David Hirsch

With Mike Cruz, the solo rider I met in Adrian, Texas, at MidPoint Cafe, the day after he made it to Chicago. The sign marks the "beginning" of Route 66.

Epilogue

One of my favorite movies is *The Bucket List* featuring Morgan Freeman and Jack Nicholson. It's an improbable story of a billionaire (Nicholson) who has all the material resources in the world, who is forced to share a hospital room with a man of very modest means (Freeman) although rich regarding family and relationships. Their very far-fetched journey, checking off their bucket list items or "things to do before they kick the bucket" takes them around the world by private jet. The journey and the movie ends at a mountain top, where their ashes are placed side by side. It's a classic for those of us in our middle years, or beyond, and I must admit I have a pretty hefty size bucket list of things I'd like to do *someday*. Doing a cross country bicycle ride was never on the list. The closest thing was, and still is, doing a cross country motorcycle trip with my boys.

The dust had hardly settled after I finished Dads Honor Ride 2015 when Peggy asked me if I would consider doing it again. I thought about it and pretty much found my answer in a fishing trip.

When young Dave was 10, we had the opportunity to go fly fishing for salmon on the Pere Marquette River just outside of Ludington, Michigan, during the annual spawn. Taking just one day, leaving Friday night after work and coming back the following evening was a big stretch for two reasons. First of all, Ludington is ten hours round trip by car. More importantly, getting a hall pass from Peggy and leaving her with the other four kids (then ages two, four, six, and eight) for an entire day would be a lot to ask.

To make a long story short, we made it up to Ludington by midnight. We met our guide at 5:30 a.m. the next morning to float and fish the Pere Marquette River for 10 hours. We hooked into more than a dozen 20–30 pound king salmon and landed one (actually truth be told it was Dave who landed the giant fish). It was one of those epic experiences for anyone who enjoys fishing. We arrived home by 9:30 p.m. Dave was very well rested having slept most of the way back. I was barely able to stay awake the last couple hours of the long drive home.

The picture of him struggling to hold the fish, before releasing it, with his ear to ear smile serves as a daily reminder of that classic father-son fishing experience.

Once the dust settled at home after the fishing trip, Peggy asked "do you think it was worth driving for ten hours and would you do it again?" While it was a very satisfying experience, I had to admit it was really a stretch. "If we were to do it again, I would fish for two days on both Saturday and Sunday. As for doing it again, let's wait and see what's going on this time next year."

Roll the clock forward, young Dave is now 26 and we've been doing the same father son fishing trip for 18 years, including his younger brother Charlie and with dozens of other dads and their boys.

When I finished the Dads Honor Ride 2015, I took the same approach that I did when hanging up the "Gone Fishing" sign all those years ago. Peggy asked if I would do it again, if the ride was worth it. For sure I would not do the same ride, Route 66 from Santa Monica to Chicago. With the benefit of hindsight, you don't have to ride 2,300+ miles to get your message out about the issue of father absence. Plus, if you want to get your message out it would be helpful to travel through more densely populated areas than the great west *where there are more cacti than people.*

Shortly after completing the ride, Lon Haldeman gave me some great advice. He said let a few months go by before planning another ride. It will take that long to put the experience in perspective. So when Peggy asked, would you do another ride, I simply said "let's wait and see."

As this book is going to press, I am somewhere on the road with Dads Honor Ride 2016, a 1,500+-mile ride from Boston to Chicago. There are more than 40 riders committed to raising awareness and funds for nine charities. Will there be another DHR in 2017?

Perhaps . . .

In the meantime, you don't have to get on a bike to change your kids' lives, just be there for them *physically, emotionally, financially* and *spiritually* and the route to becoming a 21ˢᵗ Century Dad will become clear. Just be sure to always enjoy the ride!

For more information on the 21st Century Dads Foundation
or to make a donation, please go to:
www.21stCenturyDads.org

All proceeds from this book go to support the
21st Century Dads Foundation

Resources

21st Century Dads
Fathering Self-Assessment Tool

The 21CD Fathering Self-Assessment Tool is designed to provide a father with immediate and confidential feedback on his fathering. Dads simply complete the survey and self-score themselves. They are asked to **Review** their responses, **Reflect** on what the scores mean, and **Resolve** to strengthen their commitment to fathering.

Please go to http://21stcenturydads.org/fathering-self-assessment to download the tool and get some immediate feedback and ideas on how to be a better dad.

Great Dads Coin

This treasured keepsake makes a great gift and can be carried around daily or proudly displayed at home or work. Available in English, Spanish and Polish.

To order one for yourself, a father, grandfather, father-figure, son or son-in-law go to <u>www.teamdad.com</u>.

The Great Dads Coin contains its own exclusive design features and elements. The circle is an ancient and universal symbol of unity. The outer ring has a continual chain link design symbolizing the everlasting and interlocking connection a father shares with his child. On the face and around the perimeter are the core values every Great Dad possesses: Love, Honesty, Patience and Commitment. The numbers 2-4-7-3-6-5 represent the daily, weekly, and year-long commitment Great Dads make. The bald eagle represents protection and guardianship. The banner includes the phrase *magna pater*, which is Latin for "Great Dad." In the center is a Heart, the universal symbol of love.

On the reverse and around the perimeter is the phrase "Great Dads Are Present Physically, Emotionally and Spiritually." While society puts a high price tag on dads supporting their children financially, it's equally, if not more important, for dads to have a meaningful physical, emotional and spiritual presence in their children's lives.

"What My Father Means to Me"
Me & My Dad Essay Booklet

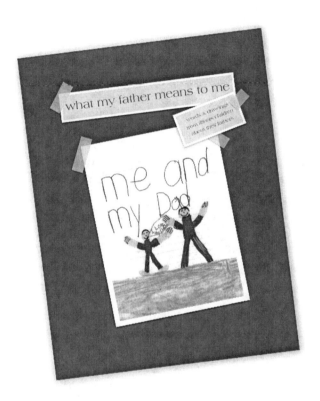

"What My Father Means to Me" is a representative collection of children's essays and drawings from the "Father of the Year" contests held in Illinois since 1997 and sponsored by Illinois Fatherhood Initiative. The essays included here have been selected from more than 400,000 entries received from communities across Illinois from both public and private schools. There is also a seven-session curriculum in the back of the booklet that provides the reader with directions to **Read** certain essays, **Reflect** on what these students have to say and **Resolve** to be a more engaged father.

To obtain a copy, please send an email to:
information@2stCenturyDads.org.

Organizations

Here are the names and contact information of the fatherhood organizations mentioned within these pages and supported by proceeds from this book and by your donations.

21st Century Dads Foundation
1515 S. Grove Avenue, #3667
Barrington, IL 60010
www.21stCenturyDads.org

All Pro Dads
5509 W. Gray Street, #100
Tampa, FL 33609
www.allprodad.com

Boot Camp For New Dads
15375 Barranca Parkway, C107
Irvine, CA 92618
www.bootcampfornewdads.org

Illinois Fatherhood Initiative
1 N. Dearborn Street, #1000
Chicago, IL 60602
www.4fathers.org

Million Father March
3509 S. King Drive, Suite 2B
Chicago, IL 60653
www.blackstarproject.org

Native American Fatherhood & Families
Association
1215 East Brown Road
Mesa, AZ 85203
www.nativeamericanfathers.org

The Tato.Net Initiative
Fatherhood Center
St. Cyril & Methodius Foundation
20-806, Lublin, ul. ks.
W. Danielskiego 10, Poland
www.tato.net

Watch D.O.G.S.
(Dads Of Great Students)
1600 West Sunset Avenue, Suite B
Springdale, AR 72762
www.fathers.com/watchdogs

21ˢᵗ Century Dads Foundation

Mission Statement

Improving the lives of children by raising awareness and resources for greater father involvement; and inspiring dads to be present—physically, emotionally, financially and spiritually.

21st Century Dads Foundation
www.21stCenturyDads.org

All proceeds from this book go to
support organizations that support kids & dads.

About the Authors

DAVID A. HIRSCH is the father of five young adults and works full-time as a wealth advisor for UBS Financial Services in Chicago. He is founder of 21st Century Dads Foundation whose mission is: *Improving the lives of children by raising awareness and resources for greater father involvement, and inspiring dads to be present; physically, emotionally, financially and spiritually.* He also is founder of the 19-year-old Illinois Fatherhood Initiative, the country's first state-wide nonprofit fatherhood organization, whose mission is: *Connecting Children & Fathers and Actively engaging fathers in the education of children.* He gave a *TEDx Talk* entitled "Why We Need to Break the Cycle of Father Absence." He has appeared on ABC, CBS, NBC, WGN as well as *The Oprah Winfrey Show.* He earned his MBA from the J.L. Kellogg Graduate School of Management at Northwestern University, and a Bachelors of Science in Accounting from the University of Illinois Urbana-Champaign. He was a national Fellow with W.K. Kellogg Foundation. He also serves on a number of boards including the Barrington Area Community Foundation and Chicago Police Memorial Foundation. David is the father of five grown children. He and his wife, Peggy, live in the Chicago area.

JOHN ST. AUGUSTINE is the author of *Living an Uncommon Life: Essential Lessons from 21 Extraordinary People* and *Every Moment Matters: Savoring the Stuff of Life*. A multi-award–winning talk radio host and producer, he is currently host of a weekly podcast called *Life Matters* on CBS digital Play.it and a sought-after speaker on human empowerment and potential. John is the father of two grown children, Amanda Lee and Andrew John. He lives in Chicago.

CPSIA information can be obtained at www.ICGtesting.com
Printed in the USA
LVOW10s2211070616

491661LV00032B/896/P